Praise for
Year-Round Indoor Salad Gardening

"*Year-Round Indoor Salad Gardening* is *not* your father's garden book. This book presents a new way to grow salad greens that doesn't require a greenhouse or grow tunnel or cold frame or sprouting jars. Step by step, in clear prose with helpful photographs, Peter Burke shows you how to grow an amazing range of greens and gives you tasty hints on how to use what you've grown. Buy this book and use it. You won't regret adding it to your garden library."

—EDWARD C. SMITH, author of *The Vegetable Gardener's Bible*

"Astounding and important, simple and doable. Every dollar you invest in Peter Burke's book can be returned to your pocket by next week."

—SHANNON HAYES, author of *Radical Homemakers*

"*Year-Round Indoor Salad Gardening* is proof that you don't need a lot of space, time, or resources to produce nutrient-dense food for you and your family. Peter Burke has written a comprehensive yet easy-to-follow guide to growing real food indoors. His soil sprouts method redefines the word 'garden.'"

—BEN HEWITT, author of *The Nourishing Homestead*

"*Year-Round Indoor Salad Gardening* offers an empowering path to growing food in any season and any living space, no matter the size or location. As a longtime grower of soil-sprouted greens, I appreciate Peter Burke's easy-to-understand style of teaching the basics. His book opens the door to an accessible way of integrating high-vibrational produce into our daily lives. This is an essential book for deepening our practices of self-reliance for greater quality of life."

—KATRINA BLAIR, author of *The Wild Wisdom of Weeds*

"Not just another sprouting book! Peter Burke offers new information that will inspire would-be sprouters, who never got started due to lack of space or time, as well as veteran growers of sprouts. This book is the answer for those who desire a fast crop with the least amount of effort, equipment, and expense. I'm sold! I'm dusting off my windowsills now."

—NOMI SHANNON, creator of RawGourmet.com
and author of *What Do Raw Fooders Eat?*

"*Year-Round Indoor Salad Gardening* is thorough and concisely written, making it a highly useful guide for both novice and advanced gardeners. Peter Burke's straightforward instructions are easy to understand and provide clear insight on how to produce an abundance of fresh soil-sprouted greens at any time of year. A helpful and inspiring resource for the inquisitive gardener."

—STEVE RODRIGUE, crop specialist for Johnny's Selected Seeds

"*Year-Round Indoor Salad Gardening* is for anybody interested in eating local food; how much more local does it get than your windowsill? It is for anyone who wants to grow fresh greens in the winter. It is for anyone who likes a bargain; you spend pennies for greens that you could spend many dollars on. It is for anyone who is interested in eating greens for health; these sprouts are packed with health-promoting substances. It is for anyone who already gardens and for those who think they can't. Peter Burke makes growing easy and puts eating local, healthy, delicious food within everyone's reach. This book is a game changer. I love it."

—DR. CLAUDIA WELCH, author of
Balance Your Hormones, Balance Your Life

"Peter Burke's book is a great resource for growing indoor salad greens. The chapters are set up in a simple sequence that is easy to follow. The excellent photos help to show what you should expect along the way. I have been using Peter's method to teach my students how to grow indoor salad greens, and it's also an excellent way to teach students of any age about sustainability, soil nutrition, and healthy eating, as well as basic plant requirements such as water, sunlight, and nutrients. Students love to grow soil sprouts because the results are so fast—and delicious!"

—STEVEN COLANGELI, science and agriculture teacher
at Middlebury Union High School, Vermont

Year-Round Indoor
Salad Gardening

Year-Round Indoor Salad Gardening

How to Grow Nutrient-Dense, Soil-Sprouted Greens in Less Than 10 Days

 **PETER BURKE**

Chelsea Green Publishing
White River Junction, Vermont

Developmental Editor: Makenna Goodman
Project Manager: Patricia Stone
Copy Editor: Deborah Heimann
Proofreader: Brianne Bardusch
Indexer: Shana Milkie
Designer: Melissa Jacobson

Printed in the United States of America.
First printing August, 2015.
10 9 8 7 6 5 4 3 2 1   15 16 17 18

Our Commitment to Green Publishing

Chelsea Green sees publishing as a tool for cultural change and ecological stewardship. We strive to align our book manufacturing practices with our editorial mission and to reduce the impact of our business enterprise in the environment. We print our books and catalogs on chlorine-free recycled paper, using vegetable-based inks whenever possible. This book may cost slightly more because it was printed on paper that contains recycled fiber, and we hope you'll agree that it's worth it. Chelsea Green is a member of the Green Press Initiative (www.greenpressinitiative.org), a nonprofit coalition of publishers, manufacturers, and authors working to protect the world's endangered forests and conserve natural resources. *Year-Round Indoor Salad Gardening* was printed on paper supplied by QuadGraphics that contains at least 10% postconsumer recycled fiber.

Library of Congress Cataloging-in-Publication Data

Burke, Peter, 1950– author.
 Year-round indoor salad gardening : how to grow nutrient-dense,
soil-sprouted greens in less than 10 days / Peter Burke.
    pages cm
 Includes index.
 ISBN 978-1-60358-615-3 (pbk.) — ISBN 978-1-60358-616-0 (ebook)
1. Salad greens. 2. Indoor gardening. I. Title. II. Title: How to grow
nutrient-dense, soil-sprouted greens in less than 10 days.

 SB351.S25B87 2015
 635'.5—dc23
                  2015013330

Chelsea Green Publishing
85 North Main Street, Suite 120
White River Junction, VT 05001
(802) 295-6300
www.chelseagreen.com

Contents

Introduction

⁕

This book is full of only good news. In a few simple steps you can grow all the fresh salad greens you need for the winter months or throughout the entire year without a lot of special equipment. No lights, no pumps, no greenhouse needed. You probably already have most of what you need to get started, without even realizing it. More good news is that you can do this for a fraction of the cost of buying fresh greens from the market! As we struggle to find ways to change course from a consumer society to a sustainable society, here is one small step we all can make and be rewarded for the effort. I have seen it over and over in my classes, the excitement of gardeners who now know they can grow fresh greens every single day. I know it well because I am right there with them. And it is good news.

From spring to fall I harvest a wide variety of salad greens from my garden—baskets of spinach in early spring, handfuls of tender young dill, tender Bibb lettuce leaves, snippets of mesclun, claytonia, corn salad, arugula. Adding to the leaves we have sugar snap peas, radishes, and early carrots, sweet and crisp. In the warmth of summer we harvest iceberg, romaine, Red Sails, and a variety of other lettuces to fill the salad bowl. By the end of summer we are eating salads of cucumber, tomato, peppers, and scallions. Good salad greens are like an artist's palette of color to make delicious and beautiful salads. In the winter by contrast, sadly I am left with what is offered at the market and our coop. Grocers certainly do their best to offer salad greens in the winter, but even at their best the offerings are weeks old and have traveled many miles by the time they get to the store. Often enough the leaves are browning at the edges by the time I get them home from the store, or they have started to wilt in their plastic clam-shell containers. I notice that with the freshness goes the flavor!

I think that the best ingredient in any kind of salad is freshness. And that is what I miss the most in the winter—big bowls of fresh greens. Well, good news: *Year-Round Indoor Salad Gardening* is going to fill your salad bowl with the freshest and most delicious greens you could want any time of year. No kidding, and that is more good news.

Gardening and growing my own food or knowing who is growing it has become an important part of my daily life. It is not as much a change as a return, a return by choice, to a more grounded way of life. From e-mail messages I get from folks across the United States—and also from Asia, Australia, the United Kingdom, the Netherlands, Puerto Rico, and Canada—I see the desire to return to the land and live a more sustainable lifestyle, if only by growing a tray of greens in an apartment window. It is good news.

Do not underestimate what that one tray growing on a windowsill can produce. If one thousand people planted one tray every day for a year, it would be equivalent to an acre of cropland yielding over two million pounds of fresh greens! It is my cherished hope that we can have acres of trays growing fresh greens on kitchen windowsills in every city or village both for the good, healthy, nutrient-rich foods they will provide, as well as for the movement this will bring toward more decentralized food production. It is kind of neat to think that people living in apartments in a big city can be part of an agrarian society by growing all their own fresh greens. More good news.

I have attempted to offer what I call multiple accesses into this book. You can read from page 1 and get the whole story. You can leaf through the book and just look at the pictures to get the "picture," or you can turn to the Quick Start Guide (on page 49) and never read another word but just start planting. And you can visit the website www.thedailygardener.com to see even more information and videos. I have tried to make it so one way or another you get what you need to do year-round indoor salad gardening.

PART I

Fresh Greens All Year

The Incredible, Edible Indoor Salad Garden

CHAPTER 1

Fresh Greens in 7 Days: An Introduction

There was a time, bookmarked in my memory, when I looked around my home and realized that the house I lived in—full of salad greens—was also my greenhouse. I was making use of a resource I never even knew I had. It was a warm place with plenty of light and plenty of water, and my plants liked to grow there. My greenhouse is a house full of greens. This book is about that realization, how I got there, and how you can grow an indoor salad garden, too.

What's on the Windowsill?

At my house when we gather around the kitchen table with friends and family, some folks eye the salad bowl with curiosity and others look on with downright suspicion. My wife and three boys are used to the unusual greens that are part of our daily fare. They've seen it all before. But for the newcomer to our table there are surprises in that bowl.

Most newcomers have seen and used alfalfa sprouts or even mung bean sprouts before, but the soil-grown sprouts from sunflower, radish, buckwheat, pea, and broccoli are unusual and new. On any particular day we might be serving an all sprout salad; on another it could be my Sunflower Caesar Salad, with sunflower greens, romaine lettuce, and parmesan cheese. Or I might make a salad with everything I have that's ready: sunflower greens, buckwheat lettuce, pea shoots, several types of radish greens, purple

This tossed salad is all soil-grown sprouts. My children gave it a thumbs-up because it looked and tasted like their idea of a regular tossed salad. Everything but the avocado was grown in my kitchen.

From left, broccoli, buckwheat, radish, peas, and sunflower on the cutting board. This is my daily harvest from five small 3 inch by 6 inch (7.5 cm × 15.2 cm) trays that were planted about seven days ago. It is a phenomenal harvest of about 14 ounces (414 g) of greens.

kohlrabi, canola, leaf lettuce, and baby spinach. My son refers to the different greens in the salad as layers: "How many layers in this one, Dad?"

The other day we made stir-fried pea shoots and garlic served with rice. It's a recipe from a friend in China, where pea shoots are called *dou miao* and they've been eating this vegetable for thousands of years.

The really remarkable thing about our salad greens is that they were all grown indoors, on a windowsill, in a week's time. And they were all harvested just before we started cooking dinner.

Growing sprouts in soil started as a winter project for me. Now I grow these delicious greens year-round. I call them "soil sprouts" to emphasize the fact that they are different from the sprouts grown in jars or microgreens grown in soil. I will go into more details on the difference between soil sprouts, sprouts, and microgreens in chapter 5, but let me say now that the soil allows the greens to grow taller and straighter and encourages the greens to leaf out more fully, it makes them easier to care for day to day, and best of all they're ready for harvest in about a week. Let me repeat that: From the time I plant the seeds to the time I harvest them is seven to ten days—about a week.

And growing these salad greens in my indoor garden keeps me gardening throughout the long Vermont winters without a greenhouse or a cold frame. It's also a great way to fill in between crops during the spring, summer, and fall gardening months. Now, of course, everyone says, "Where are the sprouts?" when I take a week off, even in summer.

My indoor salad garden in midwinter. Outside the garden is covered in snow and dormant for months, but inside my garden is growing in the short winter daylight.

My son helps with planting; it only takes a few minutes. Planting a little every day or so makes the work simple and easy. This approach means you can have a garden; just use the small spaces around your house. My greenhouse is a house full of greens!

Fresh Salad Greens Every Day

Soil sprout gardens fit into a small space and are similar to container gardening. No matter what size home you live in, there's room for a garden of soil sprouts. With nothing more than a shelf and a windowsill, you can create a productive garden indoors. Even a north-facing window is a sufficient light source—you don't need much light to green up soil sprouts. The general rule is "if you can see," it is enough light for soil sprouts. That is a stark contrast to the need for a bright southern window or even grow lights to grow microgreens. So any room with a window is fine for soil sprouts. The short growing cycle makes them easy to grow in manageable batches, even planting and harvesting small amounts every day. Freshness is guaranteed when you harvest only minutes before you serve.

It makes for easy storage, too. If you're growing for daily greens, you don't even need storage! Just cut the greens and put

There are two small trays of buckwheat sitting in the beautiful ceramic planter next to an aloe plant on the left. The productive trays of greens fit in and around regular houseplants.

them in the salad bowl! Remember the recipe for cooking sweet corn that's frequently attributed to George Washington? "First boil the water, then pick the corn." Well the same principle goes for soil sprout salads: First make the salad dressing, then cut the greens. It's a recipe for freshness, but if you do harvest more than you can use, the greens store well in the refrigerator. Still I cut just what I need and let the rest of the shoots continue to grow right in their tray. They'll grow well there for about fourteen days in all, until the first true leaves form, when they must be harvested or most of them will become bitter.

Your local food coop might have these gourmet greens available in the produce section, so if you haven't seen them yet, take a peek and try them out. You'll get a sneak preview of the homegrown goodness you're about to experience when you grow your own soil sprouts. (But chances are they won't be as fresh or as delicious.) If you've got eager, very young gardeners around, they'll get a kick out of soil sprouts, too. Every day they'll observe interesting developments under the tray covers as the sprouts grow in the dark or green up on a windowsill.

For you health-conscious gardeners out there (I'm one, too), it's good to know that during the first seven days of growth, the shoot holds the highest concentration of just about everything a plant has to offer nutritionally, and in one of the most digestible forms, so soil sprouts offer extra value, when compared with the more commonly found microgreens, or even a salad of baby mesclun or spinach that was harvested many days ago. The starch and protein in the seed become simple sugars, enzymes, amino acids, and chlorophyll. Radish soil sprouts exhibit vitamin C levels comparable to citrus fruit. But we already know that green leafy vegetables are good for us, don't we? Mom told us so!

CHAPTER 2
Genesis of the Method

Although the idea of growing immature greens to eat is nothing new, the methods outlined in this book are unique and tailored for a home garden. This chapter explains why and how I developed these simple steps to grow abundant crops of fresh greens.

Fall and the Moody Blues

I love to garden. It's been both a hobby and a passion of mine for years. Over time I've noticed that the end of the garden season and the approach of fall brings with it a bittersweet mood. It's sweet with the generous harvest and months of fresh food and bitter with the prospect of a long winter ahead without the garden.

The garden is covered in snow outdoors. It was the moody blue feeling of the approach of a long winter that was the inspiration for my research on soil sprouts.

It was during one of these melancholy fall moods that I decided to see if I could continue gardening through the coming winter months. I focused on growing fresh greens because this was garden produce that wasn't in my pantry, and my family loves big salads. We have many vegetables canned, frozen, dehydrated, and stored for use over the winter, but there's no good way to store fresh greens from the summer's outdoor harvest.

I looked at available options for growing greens in the off-season, which in Vermont means roughly October through April. Greenhouses, plastic hoop houses, and cold frames were options for extending the outdoor season. A greenhouse was beyond my budget, and cold frames needed too much daily attention for my busy work schedule. I tried a hoop house with some success, but it wasn't really what I wanted. I explored other options and decided to focus more on an indoor garden versus outdoor season extenders.

Indoor garden techniques I came across ranged from serious hydroponics in cabinets with lights and pumps to the other extreme of simple sprout jars. Hydroponics looked interesting, but I was concerned about the cost of equipment, using electric lights, and the space requirements, not to mention complicated recipes for a growing medium and nutrient formulas. The option also seemed geared more for growing out-of-season

After the fall harvest our pantry is full of canned and dried foods from the garden. The baskets are full of potatoes and onions. With the freezer and root cellar full, the only thing missing was fresh greens. Not anymore.

vegetables like tomatoes and less for growing greens. I considered a variety of other techniques and finally decided to get specific about what I *wanted* from an indoor garden first. I gave myself a challenge—to compile a wish list of sorts that I could use as a yardstick to measure my results and help focus the search.

Indoor Garden Challenge—Defining Your Wish List

Having narrowed the indoor garden challenge to growing fresh greens, I made a list of criteria that seemed reasonable to me. Well maybe I went beyond reasonable and just made a wish list. And why not?

First, I knew I wanted a productive garden. Not a toy garden, but something I could rely on to provide a quantity of daily salad greens. And I hoped this productive garden could be grown without a lot of expensive equipment. You might call me cheap, but I didn't see the sense in spending a lot of money on equipment to harvest a head of lettuce every now and then.

The next consideration on my list was the time factor: Could I create a productive indoor garden that didn't cost much to set up and only required a few minutes a day, like my earth garden outdoors? The fourth item was important: Could I grow indoors with organic methods? I didn't want to use chemical fertilizers to grow indoors. I only use organic methods in my earth garden, and it was critical for me to continue this practice indoors.

These four items would be challenge enough, but I wasn't done yet. It was a wish list after all. With my family in mind I also hoped for a method that would work well in an apartment, condominium, or dorm room, not just in my homestead kitchen. And while I was making this wish list, I decided I wanted a wide variety of fresh greens, as well. I like a salad bowl with variety.

To make things a little more complicated, I was hoping for greens that I could cook with—greens to use in a stir-fry, for instance. And the techniques for this indoor gardening needed to be easy. Easy to learn and easy to do.

The really tricky item on the list was fast growth. The quickest growing greens I knew of were mesclun lettuce mixes, but those take about 4 weeks before they're ready to harvest; I was hoping to do better. Finally, I wanted an indoor garden to be like my outdoor garden in the way that it's part of my relaxation routine—a way to unwind and feel connected after a long day at the office. It is a kind of symbiotic relationship: I nurture the garden soil and plants, and somehow I come away feeling nurtured.

My wish list for indoor gardening ultimately looked like this:

1. Productive, not a toy garden
2. Cheap, not a lot of equipment
3. Time in minutes, not hours
4. Organic methods, same as my earth garden
5. Small space, to fit indoors
6. Variety of greens
7. Greens for cooking
8. Easy-to-master techniques
9. Rapid growth, measured in days not weeks
10. Nurturing, same as my earth garden outdoors

The result of this wish list is the foundation for this book and the genesis of my indoor salad gardening methods. As I look at the list in retrospect, it seems like a tall order; I wonder how I ever thought it could be done.

Checklist: Wishes Do Come True

To answer the challenges I'd given myself required a lot of trial and error. It sometimes seemed like more error than trial. For months my house was full of indoor garden experiments. Different types of trays, a wide variety of seeds, soils and soil mixes by the cart load, and lots of planting techniques being tested. I tried some salad greens and mixes that I grow in my outdoor garden. I tried things like radishes, too—the fastest growing vegetables in the garden. In the end I used a technique I'd learned years ago: growing sprouted seeds in shallow trays of soil, in contrast to growing them in jars, the way alfalfa sprouts are grown.

A very productive square foot of trays will produce an annual yield of 54 to 72 pounds (24.4–32.6 kg) of fresh greens from eight small trays depending on which seeds are grown. At 43,560 square feet (4,047 m²) an acre of trays would yield 2,352,240 pounds (1,065,564.7 kg) of greens (over 1,000 tons) with the low estimate. Don't let the small size of the trays fool you; it is easy to grow all the salad greens you need every day.

These soil sprouts are grown for their stem and the first leaves of the plant. Rapid growth and a large seed leaf are the objectives, and only certain seed varieties work well for this method. My indoor "garden plot" evolved into a cupboard and a windowsill.

Growing Soil Sprouts by the Numbers

One square foot of trays, eight small trays, will yield about 1½ to 2 pounds (680.4–907.2 g) of sprouts every 10 days, depending on which seed varieties you grow. That adds up to an annual yield of 54 to 72 pounds (24.4–32.6 kg) of fresh greens from these eight small trays measuring 3 inches by 6 inches (7.6 cm × 15.2 cm)—my standard small tray. My indoor salad garden includes five trays (just about one half of a square foot) planted every day with five seed varieties, one variety per tray.

My yield from the five trays is about 12 to 16 ounces (340.2–453.6 g) a day. Harvested every 10 days, that yields 33 pounds (14.9 kg) of greens per year. But I plant five trays *every day* so the yield adds up to 270 pounds (122.3 kg).

These may be the most productive per-square-foot harvest on earth. But it's the simple fact that they need nothing—no greenhouse, no lights, no acres of farmland, no tractors or tillers, no plastic sheets, and almost no additional cost—beyond a few trays and some water that makes the yields really astonishing.

Using a standard measure for crop yields, pounds of produce per acre, I figure that 43,560 square feet (4,047 m²) per acre multiplied by 54 pounds (24.4 kg) per square foot per year equals an astonishing 2,352,240 pounds (1,065,564.7 kg) of produce per acre, per year (and 3,136,320 pounds [1,420,753 kg] for the more productive shoots).

So you see what I mean? No one would line up that many trays, but this little math exercise illustrates just how productive these tiny trays are by comparison to a conventional farm or garden.

That begs the question: How many people would we need to plant this hypothetical acre of trays growing greens? The answer is astonishingly few; it would only take one thousand people planting one tray a day to grow and harvest an acre of greens. Or if they planted like me it would only require two hundred people planting five trays a day to do the same thing. Why is this number important, and what relevance does it have for us today? It means that with the participation of a relatively small number of people, we could grow an acre of greens on windowsills. But further—with a simple method we could expand our cropland, so to speak, to grow an enormous harvest in our city apartments and country kitchens and sidestep the need to ship greens across the country in refrigerated trucks. This would be one step closer to a more local, sustainable food network with minimal investment. Kind of cool, right?

Looking at the wish list and taking each of my criteria for a successful indoor garden one by one shows you how I managed to get exactly what I was looking for.

Wish #1: Productive, Not a Toy Garden

I found that growing a few trays of soil sprouts provided enough greens to make a salad every day. I regularly harvested 12 to 16 ounces (340.2–453.6 g) of a variety of sprouts, and whether I added them to other greens from the market or just had an all sprout salad, there were plenty of greens. I can say that growing soil sprouts is productive enough to provide ample fresh greens for a household. This harvest came from less than one square foot of "garden space," an area that would be about the equivalent of three red bricks (96 square inches / 619 cm²). Number one on my list got a big check mark.

Wish #2: Cheap, Not a Lot of Equipment

The way I grow soil sprouts is simple. Most of the tools and equipment for indoor gardening are things I already have around the house, things like trays, soil, newspaper, and seeds. Seeds are the primary expense of indoor salad gardening and the one thing you will need to buy. Even with the expense of the seeds (plan to plant about 5 tablespoons [74 ml] of seeds a day), the average cost is well under $2.00 per pound for fresh greens. Right now in the produce section of our local supermarket, fresh greens are about $10.00 a pound, and I've seen pea shoots at the market for $25.00 a pound. That's a $23.00 difference from buying shoots versus growing your own!

Make Money the "New Fashioned Way": Grow It!

Buy seeds and *more than* double your money in less than 2 weeks. Money may not grow on trees, but it definitely grows in trays. Cost savings are significant when you grow your own fresh salad greens.

I've calculated the price per pound of pea shoots and sunflower greens. Consider: Measure seeds by volume and not by weight. A 3½-cup (828.8 ml) jar of peas is enough to plant fifty-six trays, about a 2-month supply. The seeds cost roughly $6.00 when bought in this quantity. (Buying a 50-pound bag [22.6 kg] or larger saves even more, but most folks don't have an appropriate storage space to keep that volume of seeds from losing their viability.)

The fifty-six trays together will yield about 10¾ pounds (4.9 kg) of greens. The trays, soil, and fertilizer together cost about $0.17 per tray, or $9.66 for all fifty-six trays. The trays themselves are reusable, so their cost per planting is just pennies. The soil and fertilizer are also reusable, but I put them in my outdoor garden, so I calculate them as expendables.

The total cost for 3 ounces (85 g) of pea shoots every day for 2 months is $21.60, based on a yield of 10¾ pounds (4.9 kg). That comes to $2.01 per pound of fresh greens. Pea shoots at the local market this year range between $21.00 to $25.00 per pound, so the same greens would cost $225.00 to $268.00 to buy.

Using similar calculations for sunflower greens the cost per pound comes to $1.54. The same greens at the store would be $21.00 per pound; that is if you can find these gourmet greens!

Consider, too, that these greens are 100 percent usable. When you buy lettuce at the market, the first thing you do is wash it and cut off the unusable parts. That brings the cost per pound significantly higher for store-bought greens.

I'm using high-end costs and low-end yields to demonstrate that savings are good even in the worst cases. And I haven't included the extra nutrition value of soil sprouts over lettuce or how much fun it is to have growing plants surround you in the winter months, cheering up the house or apartment. These are your bonus checks.

There's a huge cost benefit in growing your own greens, so for number two on the wish list, a cheery check mark. The return on investment for an indoor salad garden is better than the stock market! Here's a tip: Buy seeds to grow your own fresh greens, and more than double your money in 7 days.

Wish #3: Time, in Minutes Not Hours

This one is really important to me. I work a 50-hour week and have kids in school, so available time to garden is strictly limited. My earth garden is as simple as can be and only requires minutes a day from me to be productive. For my indoor garden a simple routine of planting small batches lets me grow a bountiful harvest of greens daily with a minimum of time required, easily fitting into the normal chaos of family life. Number three, check, with a sigh of relief. I'm glad to get so much in return for those few minutes.

In Minutes

It takes about 15 minutes a day to plant five trays. To water a tray of growing greens on the windowsill takes moments, not even a minute. Cutting and cleaning is measured in minutes, too, but that's something you do even with greens you buy.

So for about 15 to 20 minutes a day, you can harvest a pound of greens on a regular basis. One of my students said pea shoots at her market sell for $25.00 a pound. So you could say you're making $100.00 an hour growing pea shoots on your windowsill. It's worth the time, and it's fun, too.

Wish #4: Organic Methods, Same as My Earth Garden

I found that a simple potting soil mix, augmented with small amounts of compost and dried seaweed meal or liquid sea kelp, is all that soil sprouts need to flourish. All of these ingredients are approved for organic gardens. So item number four passed the test. One more check mark to the list. The good news is that after harvesting the greens the leftover mass of roots and soil is a great addition to a compost pile and can even be reused for indoor salad gardening or in a regular outdoor garden.

Wish #5: Small Space, to Fit Indoors

What I found was that I only needed a cupboard and a windowsill for a productive indoor salad garden. The garden fits right into an apartment or a homestead kitchen—no huge space requirements or special additions to the house are involved. Number five on the wish list, check. I still marvel at how simple it is to find the necessary room, and over the years of teaching these techniques to others, I've been amazed at the many creative solutions I've seen people come up with to create their own indoor salad garden.

Wish #6: Variety of Greens

I started with five varieties of seed that are the basis of my soil sprout garden. I've added more choices (about twenty at last count) over the years, and the wide range of combinations makes for beautiful-looking and delicious tossed salads. Number six, check.

Wish #7: Greens for Cooking

Most of the greens from soil sprouts are best used fresh, but pea shoots are terrific cooked; I even noticed a recipe in *EatingWell Magazine* that suggested using pea shoots. I include pea shoots and broccoli soil sprouts in tempura with great success, and I add chopped broccoli sprouts to my soups as a garnish for added flavor and nutrition. Item number seven is another check mark on the list.

I find growing fresh greens to cook with is particularly satisfying. I had thought it would be impossible to accomplish, but of course the Chinese were about 3,000 years ahead of me. (See recipes, chapter 16.)

Wish #8: Easy-to-Master Techniques

Indoor salad gardening is easy to learn. In fact I have seen kids grow fantastic gardens after only one demonstration. By following the instructions in this book, you will be harvesting fresh, lush greens about this time next week.

It's easy to adjust what you grow to fit the needs of your family or household. The routine for planting and watering is simple, taking only a few minutes a day. This type of growing is perfect for the gardener's kitchen in every way, and it's easy to plan your harvest—it's only 7 to 10 days

An indoor salad garden requires a dark place to start the seeds for the first 4 days, what I call the incubation period. This simple step makes a tremendous difference in both the quality of the greens and the quantity of the harvest. My warm, dark place is the cupboard over our refrigerator.

away! I especially like the instructions for the first 4 days of sprouting: *Do nothing*. That's a cinch to follow. Item eight, check.

Wish #9: Rapid Growth, Measured in Days Not Weeks

This is my most prized success. These greens are ready to harvest 7 to 10 days after planting. There was no other technique that compared to this. Nothing came close to a 1-week cycle of planting and harvest. I've tried every vegetable I could think of to find out what I could harvest in a short time and grow indoors. These greens outpaced every one of them. Wish list item number nine, double check, exclamation point.

Wish #10: Nurturing, Same as My Earth Garden Outdoors

Garden work is a bit like alchemy for me. I suppose like any good hobby, when all is said and done, you feel better afterward by the doing. Like whittling a pipe or building a table, you have something of value at the end, but part of the reward is in the doing. This was true for my indoor garden. Planting, watering, harvesting, and making great meals with soil sprouts give the same sense of satisfaction I get from my earth garden. Number ten was a huge success for me and the final check mark on my list.

Looking Forward to Winter

Watering daily with small amounts of water takes just a few minutes and makes it possible to use trays without holes in the bottom, such as these ceramic bowls and cedar boxes. They require about 2 to 4 tablespoons (30–59 ml) of water daily.

Now when that first cold snap comes in the fall and I hear the geese flying south, I don't worry. No more winter blues. With the pantry full of garden harvest, I start my daily routine of growing fresh greens indoors on the windowsill. My desire to keep gardening has been realized to perfection.

This is how *Year-Round Indoor Salad Gardening* got started, with a desire to keep gardening in the winter and a wish list that I thought was impossible. During the initial experimenting, and in years of gardening indoors since then, my understanding and refinement of techniques have been honed by teaching classes to make the journey complete and satisfying.

CHAPTER 3
The Nature of Soil Sprouts Is Counterintuitive

The tricky part of growing soil sprouts is that it is so different, it runs out of bounds of most gardening common sense. It is like discovering something that is both obvious and hidden, simple yet tricky. But don't worry that it is hard to mess up. That is my motto—"you can't mess this up."

Counterintuitive Gardening

Growing soil sprouts runs counter to much of what I always held true about gardening in general. When I try to explain soil sprouts to my farming friends and gardening buddies, they often have trouble understanding the concept at first. I know what bothers them: They think that if they plant 70 sunflower seeds or 150 broccoli seeds, their crop will be enormous compared to the tray of greens I describe.

One farmer complained, "It is so seed intensive." He thought too many seeds were required, and he dismissed the idea. He reasoned that one mature sunflower could produce easily hundreds of seeds, or each full-grown plant a large head of broccoli. Why harvest the sprouts before they've had a chance to produce their full yield?

But when you look at it in a different light, it makes sense. No one would call it "seed intensive" to grind up wheat berries or corn kernels—which are viable seeds—to make bread or object to boiling rice to make dinner. Soil sprouts are just another way—a different way—to *eat seeds*. Rather than grinding or boiling I grow them for a short time. Plus many of the seed varieties that I grow for greens wouldn't be used as food themselves, like radish seeds and broccoli seeds. With my methods seeds that could only be planted in the outdoor garden in the past can now be used to grow fresh greens indoors. They've found a useful place in the pantry as winter food. An indoor salad garden can even work as a full-time garden for those who live in apartments or condominiums with no other place to grow their own food.

The staples corn, wheat, and rice. Some farmer friends complained that soil sprouts were too "seed inten-sive." But in a different light the soil sprouts are just another way—a different way—to prepare seeds to eat. Rather than boil or grind the seeds, they are *grown* for a short time.

Totally Different Techniques

The techniques that work for an indoor salad garden of soil sprouts are not the same as those I use for my earth garden. Much of what I had learned about gardening went out the window when I started this project. An indoor garden required an entirely different approach. For instance, instead of watering the seeds *after* planting, as I would normally do in my earth garden, I water the seeds *before* planting by soaking them. Where I usually plant seeds *in the soil* outdoors, for soil sprouts I scatter the seeds *on top of* the soil indoors. In my outdoor garden seeds are planted in carefully spaced patterns. For my indoor garden's soil sprouts I spread the soaked seeds on top of the soil so close together that the seeds touch.

Normally gardeners take pains to provide plenty of light for young plant starts, providing grow lights from the moment the new plants emerge from the soil. It's a totally opposite approach for soil sprouts; I start them *in the dark* for 4 days.

For the experienced gardener it's a bit of a challenge to go against the grain of years of gardening outdoors. I know it was for me. If this is your first garden and it's all new, you don't have the "this-is-how-I-usually-do-it" attitude to overcome. But I should give you fair warning that if your expert gardener friends tell you you're doing it all wrong, they would be right—that is, if you were growing outdoors!

Just be patient and invite them over for a fresh salad sometime in January, when they're frozen out of their own gardens.

Watering the Seeds First

Presoaking gives the seeds a jump start before planting. Usually seeds must soak up enough water from the soil to initiate growth. Depending on the environment it might take days before the seeds even begin to sprout. Although soaking is common to hasten the process of growth for large seeds, with soil sprouts all of the seeds are soaked first, regardless of size. This step is a key to realizing the "fast growth" found in indoor salad gardening.

Plant on Top of the Soil

Planting the seed on top of the soil also saves a day or two because the stem and leaf don't have to push up through the soil. It also prevents the seed hull and leaves from being covered in soil and keeps the sprout cleaner. Cleaner stems and leaves mean there's less of a chance the plants will develop damp off (a disease that quickly kills young shoots) or molds, and the greens are easy to clean at harvest time. If you've ever cleaned fresh greens from the garden, you'll appreciate this aspect of soil sprouts.

For the outdoor garden pea seeds would be spaced 3 inches (7.6 cm) apart and 1 inch (2.5 cm) deep. For the indoor garden many aspects are counterintuitive; in this case the seeds are touching and on top of the soil.

Seeds Are Touching

Outside I would need a 50-foot garden row to plant the same tablespoon of sunflower seeds that I use inside in a small tray that's only ⅛ of 1 square foot in size. By planting the seeds so close that they touch, I get the maximum possible harvest of greens from the smallest possible area. The seed has only enough room to send a root down into the soil and a stem up toward the light, but this is entirely adequate for the short "growing season" of shoots.

Grow in the Dark

Growing in the dark also flies in the face of everything I know about vegetable gardening. For my traditional garden I use lights and a cold frame or a greenhouse to give young plants plenty of light in the early stages. But soil sprouts are grown for the stem and first leaves of the plant only, and the first few days of darkness encourage a long stem to grow by "forcing" the seed to search for light. Outdoors, in more hostile conditions, a seed stem may have to make its way through a pile of leaves or straw before it comes out of the dark. The simulated darkness of a tray with paper covers takes advantage of this natural urge in plants to search for light. It encourages a very productive harvest. Total darkness isn't necessary (I'll get down to specifics in later chapters); even low-light conditions will do the job of forcing the sprouting seeds to develop long stems in the first stages of growth.

Plant Every Day

In my outdoor earth garden I typically plant varieties like tomatoes or squash once per season. For vegetables like lettuce and carrots I do a second planting at mid-season to harvest a fall crop. For varieties like radishes I replant every 2 weeks and enjoy a steady supply of fresh roots all growing season.

With soil sprouts I plant every day. For a steady supply of greens from my indoor salad garden, planting every day is key. I routinely start small batches of seeds, about 5 tablespoons (74 ml) spread over five trays each day. So every day a batch of seeds planted a week ago are coming to harvest. And I know just how many trays I'll need, week to week, harvesting just what I need each time. I want my indoor salad garden to remain small and manageable, not large or time consuming. Like the KISS philosophy—Keep It Simple, Stupid—I like to Keep It Small, . . . !

Harvest More from the Seed

As I explained above my objective when growing sprouts in soil is to encourage rapid growth of the stem and a large seed leaf (called a coty-ledon). This allows me to harvest nearly all of the stored nutrition from the seed. This general principle has been understood in Asia and elsewhere for many centuries. I was surprised to read an Italian recipe from the year AD 1624 that included radish sprouts, and the English have used cress sprouts for many years, too. Rich in vitamin C, cress sprouts helped sailors to combat scurvy on long voyages. For my indoor salad garden I've included a variety of seeds and developed in-depth techniques to grow soil sprouts full time.

Some mystery still remains, though, even after all these years working with seeds. I'm always excited by the miracle I witness each time I soak them for another batch of sprouts. As soon as I pour the water onto the seeds, it's off to the races, with all the potential in those little "horses" galloping to the finish line—I can almost hear the cheers!

I've learned a lot about seeds and sets from growing soil sprouts; in fact some of the techniques I've put to good use in my outdoor garden, too. Take peas, for instance. They're hardy in the cool Vermont spring, but that's truer for the plant than the seed. An early, wet spring can make for patchy germination at best, and other times the peas just rot in the soil. One early spring day a few years ago, I realized that I had all these hale and hearty pea sprouts growing indoors in trays, and I wondered, "Why not transplant them outdoors?"

They were an instant success.

I planted two rows of peas, and they had no trouble growing perfectly well, with no setback effect from transplanting. This was especially surprising. The typical book on gardening will tell you that peas do not transplant well!

For many years I have had an annual bet with a friend of mine: Whoever grows the first 3-inch pea plant wins. He categorically ruled this transplantation technique unfair. For our bet the seeds must be planted directly in the ground outdoors. Still I plant an extra-early batch of peas just for bragging rights—and for the delicious sweet peas, too. Sometimes going against the grain, stepping outside the box and doing something counterintuitive, offers rich rewards. Growing soil sprouts is one of those times.

CHAPTER 4

Ten Good Reasons to Sprout in Soil versus by Traditional Methods

S oil sprouts, microgreens, sprouts, and baby greens are all different versions of immature greens. I have tried all of these methods and more in order to come up with what I needed for year-round indoor salad greens. This chapter is a rundown of the methods I used and the reasons I chose to grow soil sprouts over all the rest.

The Benefits of Soil Grown

Some might be wondering, "Why grow sprouts in soil?" You might ask, "Why not grow sprouts in jars like everyone else?"

When I first started experimenting with indoor garden techniques, I'd already been sprouting alfalfa and mung beans in jars. Building on this I expanded the types of seeds I sprouted. I added clover, lentils, various sprout mixes, and I even tried onion seeds because catalogs listed them. I sprouted in jars, baskets, bags, and plastic sprouters, like the Biosta sprouter, all in an attempt to create an indoor garden to fill the salad bowl. One problem with these sprouts had no solution: My family was lukewarm to the salads I made. They were OK with adding sprouts to a leaf salad, and they didn't mind mung bean sprouts in a stir-fry with other vegetables, but that was enough sprouts for everyone. What I was looking for were greens I could grow and use exclusively for a tossed green salad.

I liked these early traditional sprouts, but truth be told I wasn't completely satisfied either. When I served the lush and tasty greens that grew from soil-grown sprouts, my family's reaction told the story I wanted to hear. Everyone, including the kids, enjoyed the salads. I had the variety of greens I was looking for—the soil-grown sprouts looked like regular tossed salad greens. I had achieved the look and texture I wanted.

Buckwheat and sunflower seeds drop their hulls as they grow; it is a real plus when it is time to harvest. The hulls are easy to sweep up by hand. A portable vacuum cleaner works well, too. And every time a hull drops you can relish the fact that you did not have to wash it off.

Most gurus in the field agree that sprouts grown on soil are more nutritious, too. The suggestion is that the roots can draw full nutrients from the soil, compost, and sea kelp meal continuously as they grow, even in their very short growing cycle. I haven't found any research to support this claim, but there's tons of evidence that shows soil sprouts are good food. I don't see any point in trying to make them "more better" to justify growing them on soil; there are plenty of good reasons to grow soil sprouts already! Here are my top reasons to grow this way:

1. Hulls drop off as sprouts grow

One great thing about growing soil sprouts is, there's no need to wash the hulls off the sprouts. Hulls drop off on their own as the leaves grow and spread open. With jar-grown sprouts, whether alfalfa or mung beans, washing to separate the hulls from the sprouts is a tedious job. Heaven knows I've cleaned enough of them. There are tricks to the trade, but generally it takes time to get the hulls off. No matter what you do it seems like you can't get rid of them all. Hulls mixed in with the greens tend to increase the spoilage factor and can affect the flavor of the sprouts. With soil sprouts the hulls drop off as they grow and require

The greens can be left to grow in the tray if you don't need them all for your salad. It is an alternative to cutting the whole tray and storing the extra in the refrigerator. Just remember to water the tray.

only a minimum of washing. In some cases you might get hulls that cling to the seed leaf, but it is easy to pick off the few of them that linger, and it is nothing compared to having all of the hulls mixed in with the greens.

2. You can store right in the tray

When the soil sprouts are ready they can be "stored" right in their tray for a few extra days. Just water once a day, and they stay fresh and green until you are ready to harvest. In fact, the soil sprouts continue to grow. In contrast, after a few days of storage, the tips of my jar-grown sprouts start to brown a little and the hulls tend to rot. They have to go in the fridge if I am not ready to use them right away, and even then they need regular rinsing to keep them from spoiling. And with store-bought sprouts often the roots are brown and unappealing.

3. Easy to care for

The first 4 days you do nothing with soil sprouts. They stay in the dark on a shelf or in a cupboard. Once the seeds are planted moist soil and moist paper covers make for perfect conditions for the growing seeds, no watering necessary in the initial stage. On the fifth day, when the cover comes off and the tray is in the light, you need to water only once a day. That is much easier than rinsing two or three times a day with jars, baskets, or bags.

4. Heartier greens

If you miss a watering, it's not a catastrophe with soil sprouts; there's enough moisture in the soil to carry sprouts through a day. If you really mess up and come home to limp greens, use soil sprout CPR—water the

All is not lost when you come home to find that one of the trays is wilted. You can perform sprout CPR to revive the greens. Simply water, bag, and chill.

Step one of sprout CPR is to rinse the stems and leaves with cool water and water the soil, being careful not to waterlog the soil mix.

Step two of sprout CPR is to place the whole tray in a plastic bag overnight. In hot weather put the bagged tray in the refrigerator for a few hours or overnight.

Step three of sprout CPR is to remove the plastic bag, and the revived greens are ready to go back to the windowsill or to be harvested for a salad. This revival is not something that could be done with sprouts grown in jars and is another reason to grow in soil.

tray, put it in a plastic bag, and place it in the refrigerator. This works well—they spring back to life! Not so with sprouts in a jar that spoil quickly without regular tending; there is no reviving them.

5. Creates a "greenspace"

It is great to see greens growing around the house and kitchen. Some of the seeds produce pink and purple stems and add a touch of life to the room. I sometimes put the trays in ceramic pots so I can vary the look of my indoor salad garden. Even in small trays the greens are a welcome sight and mix in well with my wife's houseplants. In the dead of winter with the greens growing, even thriving, they remind me that the cold is only for a while; soon I'll be outdoors in the garden again!

The same is true if you're in an apartment and don't have a place to grow a garden. A few trays of fresh greens help to satisfy the gardening urge and provide a greenspace to the apartment atmosphere, whereas jars or a sprouter can offer little to the indoor landscape. Growing soil sprouts in your house refreshes the air with oxygen just like regular houseplants. Could you ask for a better air freshener?

6. Visualize the harvest

Another thing I like about trays of fresh greens is that I can see what's ready to harvest, making it easy to visualize what's for dinner. I

The edible indoor salad garden gives more than just fresh greens. The beautiful, tender plants share their bright colors and help to keep the air indoors fresh with oxygen.

frequently choose the trays that I'll harvest as I water them before dinner. With the sprouts tucked away in jars, bags, and plastic trays, there's no easy way to see which ones are nearing harvest time.

7. Much faster and easier than microgreens

If you've ever grown microgreens, you know they're not ready in 7 days. If you're lucky and choose the right varieties of greens, you can harvest them in about 21 days. So in the time you could even begin to eat microgreens, you've already harvested soil sprouts three times and you're planting your fourth set of sprout trays. I figure it's possible to harvest over a pound of greens from just 1 square foot of trays every week or so. Compare that to the size of any greenhouse, cold frame, or garden plot, and you'll be clicking your heels and singing a song. Plus microgreens need added light to grow indoors; without electric grow lights microgreens get long and spindly.

8. Simpler than hydroponics

Anything that has a recirculation pump seems more like a swimming pool than a garden to me. Don't get me wrong: I like the hothouse and hydroponically grown tomatoes I buy at the store in the winter. I'm glad someone has the patience and inclination to mess with the gear. But when I look at the equipment and the list of ingredients in the growing medium, I know I don't have the time, the space, or the patience to use this technique. Just give me seeds and soil and I am all set to garden.

9. Great flavor

An all soil sprout salad is full of rich flavors and textures. Sunflower greens are crispy and have a mild nutty flavor. Buckwheat lettuce has a delicate texture and a sweet and sour flavor. Pea shoots have a sweet, pea taste. The thought of an *all* alfalfa sprout salad is not as appealing or flavorful to me. Although it's good and good for you, I guarantee my kids would look at me cross-eyed if I tried to sell it to them as a salad!

10. More color and texture

The bright-colored stems of soil sprouts make a beautiful and exciting salad mix. Bright red stems of Hong Vit radish, purple stems of the purple kohlrabi, bright pearly white of broccoli and sunflower, all combine in the salad bowl for a festival of color. Add the soft pink and sometimes deep red of buckwheat and the bright orange of a grated carrot—there's nothing like these salads.

The variety of textures, flavors, and colors from combining the different greens makes a unique, full-bodied tossed salad, a gourmet treat you get to enjoy every day.

Take your pick of reasons to grow soil sprouts. If you've been growing sprouts in jars, just the fact that you don't have to wash all those hulls will be high on your list. If you're looking for wonderful gourmet salads all winter long, the great flavors and colors of a soil sprout mix might appeal to you. Whatever your reason you're in for a treat with indoor salad gardening.

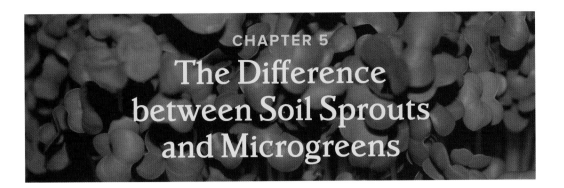

CHAPTER 5

The Difference between Soil Sprouts and Microgreens

Teaching workshops on indoor salad gardening has been a great way for me to learn from the questions folks ask during and after the sessions. I have heard a lot of confusion in terminology. This section expanded from a conversation, a series of e-mail conversations really, with my editor. I had planned to add a section on definitions of terms anyway, but our conversation highlighted the need for clarity. At one point when I said I was not going to include a chapter on microgreens, she replied, "Isn't microgreens a huge part of the book? I'm confused . . . ." After a few more e-mails I finally got it. We were using the same word for two different things. In this case she was using the word *microgreens* as a general term for growing greens, and I was using it to refer to a specific way to grow greens.

The essence of the issue is that there are a number of techniques for growing immature greens. Sprouts, bean sprouts, shoots, microgreens, baby greens, and soil sprouts are all immature greens. Each one is distinct in how it is grown and at what stage of growth it is harvested. Still, the terms are often used interchangeably to label any immature green we use for salads. I will frequently hear people say things like "Oh, you're the sprout guy!" and it would be lost on them if I corrected them by saying, "No, I am the *soil sprout and shoot* guy."

Just so we are all on the same page through the rest of the book, I'm going to make an attempt to clarify terms, realizing that these are my definitions only and not an official certified definition. I have witnessed this confusion of terminology in all types of media—radio, television, magazine articles, online articles, and even dictionaries like Wikipedia— so it stands to reason there is confusion. Let's try to clear things up.

I'll start with the basics: When a seed sprouts, it sends out a root and a stem with a seed leaf. The seed leaf is the two halves of a seed when it opens and becomes a set of leaves. Once the seed leaves spread out the first true leaf appears in the crotch of the two leaves. The true leaf resembles the leaves of the mature plant both in look and flavor. Each of the parts of a plant can be encouraged to grow in different ways using different techniques that I'll explain below. At the end of each section I'll list a few of the pros and cons. I'll compare each of these different traditional methods to growing soil sprouts, the subject of this book. Growing soil sprouts is my yardstick.

Microgreens

Microgreens are grown for the first true leaves of a plant instead of just the stem and seed leaf. It is not a distinction without a difference. The first true leaf takes a little longer to develop. The tray of sprouting seeds is introduced to a light source as soon as the seeds begin to sprout and root. When you introduce light the seed leaf spreads out near the soil and sends up the true leaf. The first true leaf looks like the plant. The seed leaf, by contrast, is not as distinct to the variety and resembles the shape of the seed itself. The flavor of microgreens is more characteristic of the mature plant. Microgreens require full sunlight, a fluorescent lightbulb, or LED grow light to grow properly; you will not be able to get a good crop with just sunlight from a windowsill.

There are a wide selection of seed varieties that can be grown for microgreens. The most commonly used varieties are arugula, broccoli, beets, cabbage, Swiss chard, kale, kohlrabi, komatsuna, mizuna, mustard, radish, basil, cilantro, celery, dill, fennel, fenugreek, salad burnet, shiso, and sorrel.

The Pros and Cons of Growing Microgreens

The pros of growing microgreens for salads are the wide variety of flavors available and the custom mixes of seeds that are unique and fun. There are a number of colors and textures as well as flavors that make a great palette for the creative cook.

The downside of growing microgreens is really a list of things. It starts with the need for lights or a greenhouse. In the winter, when you need greens the most, you need a heated greenhouse. The trays are large trays and need a lot of space to grow enough for a salad every day. It takes at least 2 weeks to grow a crop, some take longer—up to 4 weeks until harvest. Microgreens are usually grown in a standard 20-inch by 10-inch (50.8 × 25.4 cm) black plastic tray or something similar to that.

By my measurements it would require a tray per day to harvest a salad bowl of microgreens. That would require the home grower to have fourteen trays growing at all times. You would need seven 4-foot (1.2 m)

Microgreens grown in a 20-inch by 10-inch (50.8 × 25.4 cm) tray under lights.

fluorescent light fixtures or a heated greenhouse to provide a steady supply of greens. It would be very expensive to heat a greenhouse for the winter, and it would require a lot of precious indoor space to house fourteen trays.

Sprouts

Sprouts are simply seeds grown for the root, stem, and seed leaf. The most well known of all the sprouts are alfalfa sprouts. Sprouts are commonly grown in a quart Mason jar with a screen top. Seeds are soaked overnight, rinsed, and drained, then set up to allow the remaining water to drain. The jars of soaked seeds require rinsing three times a day. After the first day you can see the tails of the root appear. Within a few days the root lengthens and the seed becomes yellow leaves. Sprouts are ready in about 7 days.

The home gardener can grow sprouts using stacked plastic trays that rely on gravity to rinse the seeds. When water is poured into a top tray, it rinses and hydrates the seeds as it flows down through the trays. The bottom tray is a reservoir for the rinse water. These appliances are usually limited to three or four stacked trays.

Sprouts grown in a quart Mason jar. They need to be rinsed two to three times a day.

The harvest is the root, stem, and seed leaf about 3 or 4 inches (7.6–10.2 cm) long. They can be used with the seed leaf still yellow, although if grown in a kitchen there is usually enough light to green the tiny seed leaves. Alfalfa, clover, broccoli, radish, arugula, cress, and mustard are the most common seeds grown for sprouts.

The Pros and Cons of Growing Sprouts

The most appealing aspect of sprouts is the downright simplicity in getting started. A jar, seeds, and a piece of screen is all it takes to grow sprouts. The simplicity stops there when you consider both rinsing three times a day and a place to put all the jars for the 7 days it takes to mature to a usable size. Rinsing takes a lot of fresh water and is required morning, noon, and night, so it is a significant time commitment.

Another drawback of growing sprouts is the unforgiving nature of this technique; miss a rinsing and you have mush in a jar. The entire jar full can be lost to rot, just like that. I have verified in my classes that this is a common experience and not just my problem. It is tough to be that diligent with our busy lives.

What I use as a gauge to measure a growing technique is how much it will take to produce a salad every day that will feed four people. That is about 12 to 16 ounces (340.2–453.6 g) of finished greens. For sprouts a salad every day requires three to four jars a day times 7 days. Finding space for between twenty-one and twenty-eight jars is complicated in a small kitchen. What I hear in my classes is that most people grow a few jars of sprouts and add them to their regular salads rather than trying to find space for twenty-eight jars. Another drawback to sprouts is washing the seed hulls off the greens. I have done a lot of this, and even though I am good at it, it does take a lot of time, not to mention a lot of fresh water.

Shoots

Shoots usually describes pea shoots. They are essentially grown the same way as soil sprouts, but with peas there is no seed leaf; there is just a stem and side branches of tiny leaves. French lentil and adzuki beans are similar and can be called shoots, too. Sometimes you see corn listed with shoots in seed catalogs, but they do not make a good salad green.

The Pros and Cons of Shoots

Shoots share the same set of pros and cons as soil sprouts. One additional advantage to shoots is that they will regrow after the first cutting, although each successive cutting is smaller than the first.

Baby Greens

Baby greens are grown for full-sized true leaves of the plant but are cut before the main stems develop. They fall within the group of immature greens that fit our general description of microgreens. Lettuces are good candidates for baby greens, as are any variety of beet or Swiss chard. The hands-down favorite baby green in the United States is baby spinach. Baby greens are seeded closer than normal plantings but not as close as microgreens. They need about 40 days from planting to harvest. They are grown in greenhouses, in a raised bed in wide rows, and can be grown indoors but require lights. Just about any seed variety that works for a mesclun mix will produce baby greens. Timing a harvest is critical, so I would not recommend growing a mix of greens but instead growing each seed variety separately. That way as the baby plant grows you can cut it at just the right stage for a salad. Because of the long growing time make sure you have a deep tray of rich soil if they are grown indoors.

The Pros and Cons of Baby Greens

Baby spinach is like the Holy Grail of fresh greens. You should be able to get two cuttings from a bed or tray. For the home gardener trying to grow fresh greens in the winter is not a good choice. Baby greens require either a heated greenhouse or shelves with grow lights. To grow enough for the salad every day, about 12 to 14 ounces (340.2–396.9 g) of cut greens, the gardener would need to have about twenty 20-inch by 10-inch (50.8 × 25.4 cm) trays and ten 4-foot (1.2 m) grow lights. That's a big commitment of space and resources in a home. If it was necessary I might consider it, but the fact is, you can grow that amount of greens in a much smaller space with shoots and soil sprouts.

Soil Sprouts

Soil sprouts, as you already know by now, is my own descriptive term for sprouts grown in soil. They are grown in *soil* versus in *jars*. They are grown for the stem and seed leaf, like sprouts, but not the root. The trick to getting a productive crop is forcing the seeds in the dark for 4 days. This encourages a long stem. Once the stems are about 1 inch tall, the tray is ready to come out of the dark and into the light. The stems will continue to grow, and the seed leaves will mature for another 3 to 5 days until they are ready to cut. They are cut just above the soil line, leaving the roots in the soil. Once the greens are cut they will not grow another crop.

The Pros and Cons of Soil Sprouts

The upside of soil sprouts is the lush greens that you can harvest in a short growing season. You can grow large seeds like sunflower with the hulls or small seeds like broccoli using the same technique. Soil sprouts are very productive for the time and space involved. Watering is only once a day, and if you miss a watering, they will not rot and die. Of all the ways to grow immature greens or microgreens, this is the easiest and most productive technique.

The cons of soil sprouts are having trays and soil ready and the time it takes for the daily plantings.

Making a comparison of methods of growing immature greens is useful to us not only in highlighting my decision to grow soil sprouts, but also because it helps to define the methods and match them to what you want from an indoor garden. If you are like me and want a big pile of fresh greens every day, then growing soil sprouts is the answer for you, too.

CHAPTER 6
Becoming a Daily Gardener

When I first started to grow soil sprouts, I planted a tray of seeds and harvested the greens 7 days later, then planted another tray and harvested that tray. I thought that was great—it was fast compared to the other types of greens I grew. Those lettuce and mesclun mixes needed 21 to 28 days at least before the first harvest of baby greens. Because I wanted to harvest more greens to use over a week, I started using larger trays, about the size of a typical cafeteria tray. I reasoned that if I had a larger harvest I could store greens in the refrigerator until the next harvest.

What actually happened was a mess!

The larger trays took longer to plant and were difficult to work with at the kitchen table. I needed larger shelves to hold these trays, and the new shelves didn't look as good in the living room. The arrangement made it harder to get light to the entire tray without adding electric grow lights. On top of all that the larger trays had more trouble with damping off and molds.

They did yield a larger harvest, but there was a problem with that, too. The harvest took up too much room in the refrigerator, and the stored greens were more likely to brown or even go bad before we could eat them. I was not happy. I needed more greens but wasn't sure how to make it happen.

Then it dawned on me that I could just plant smaller trays more frequently—even every day—creating successive daily harvests. With this simple change so many things fell into place: I could plant a small tray in a minute; it was easy. I had no more trouble with molds. Small trays were great for planting right at the kitchen table. Quick setup, quick clean up, and the planted trays fit in the kitchen cupboard for their initial incubation period of 4 days in the dark.

The small trays fit easily on a windowsill, too, or on a small shelf beside a window, making it possible to green the sprouts with natural light for the final few days. I was pleased to get rid of those grow lights.

Smaller trays tuck in around other houseplants, too, becoming part of the room decor. These are just a few of the reasons I was happy with this development. I started to think big by thinking small and switching to more frequent plantings.

Think "Every Day"

Actually I had to stop thinking like a farmer. When a farmer plants a crop the plan is for a one-time harvest of a huge crop after several months of growth when the plants finally mature. A gardener plants with a similar objective, just on a smaller scale.

For indoor salad gardening to work on a small-tray scale, I had to think of my crop as a daily salad and the time to maturity as a week to 10 days—a very different outlook than I had as an outdoor gardener. With a daily routine I plant what I expect to use in one day and it's done in a few minutes using a little shelf space. I'm not planting to harvest a "crop," but rather just enough for one salad—10 to 12 ounces (283.5–340.2 g) of fresh greens. When I know family or friends are coming for dinner, it's easy to add a tray or two to the daily routine or harvest a few trays a day early.

By starting at the end, in this case knowing how much I want to harvest next week, I determine how much to plant today, tomorrow, and the next day. In 7 days the salad greens are ready to cut. Just enough. No worries about storage or spoilage.

It's like a just-in-time inventory—the greens arrive on time, when I need them, every day.

To get the particular yield I want, I plant five trays a day, one each of the most popular seeds: sunflower, radish, buckwheat, pea, and broccoli. I add two trays of peas once a week for a family favorite—stir-fry with pea shoots, mushrooms, and garlic. If it's winter and I want more greens, I add a few trays of sunflower or I add more seed varieties like purple kohlrabi, Chinese cabbage, or Hong Vit radish. These adjustments are easy to make when I have to plan only 10 days in advance.

The minimal space required by using the small trays makes it possible for someone living in an apartment, condominium, or dorm room to produce abundant fresh greens; an indoor salad garden using these small trays is not a garden only in name; it is a real, productive, feed-the-family garden.

What Do I Mean by "Small Tray"?

When I say "small tray" I'm talking about an open container measuring 3 inches wide by 6 inches long by 2 inches deep (7.6 × 15.2 × 5.1 cm); my "large tray" is 4 inches wide by 8 inches long by 2 inches deep (10.2 ×

Although I often use foil bread loaf pans for planting, there is a wide variety of trays that work just as well. These ceramic and wood, oval, round, and rectangular shapes work just as well and look nice. Calculate the amount of seeds to plant in your tray by comparing to the standard small 3-inch by 6-inch (7.6 × 15.2 cm) tray, then adjust from there.

20.3 × 5.1 cm). (When I refer to a small tray or a large tray in this book, these are the sizes I am talking about unless otherwise noted.) Depending on the circumstances I use some ceramic bowls and wooden boxes and the foil bread pans. Table 6.1 gives an idea of the amount of seeds to plant in trays of different sizes.

Table 6.1. Seed Amounts for Different-Sized Trays

Tray Size	Squared Size	Amount of Seeds
3 × 6 inches (7.6 × 15.2 cm)	18 square inches (115.5 cm^2)	1 tablespoon (14.8 ml)
4 × 8 (10.2 × 20.3)	32 (207)	2 tablespoons (29.6)
6 × 8 (15.2 × 20.3)	48 (308.6)	3 tablespoons (44.4)
8 × 8 (20.3 × 20.3)	64 (412.1)	3½ tablespoons (51.8)
4-inch round (10.2-cm round)	13 (81.7)	2 teaspoons (9.8)
5 round (12.7 round)	20 (126.6)	1⅓ tablespoons (19.7)
6 round (15.2 round)	28 (181.4)	2 tablespoons (29.6)
10 round (25.4 round)	79 (490.6)	4 tablespoons (59.2)

My garden friends poke fun at me, saying I'm no longer square foot gardening (outdoors, I use the Square Foot Gardening method popularized by Mel Bartholomew), I'm *square inch* gardening. The truth is, these may be the most productive square inches in the gardening world. I average yields of about 2 to 3 ounces (56.7–85.1 g) of greens from each small tray weekly. I know it doesn't sound like much, but if I plant four trays a day and harvest the low average of 2 ounces (56.7 g) of greens from each one, that comes to about 4 pounds (1.8 kg) of greens a week. Those 4 pounds are grown on only ½ of 1 square foot of garden space! And that's the low estimate. I routinely harvest more, depending on the seed variety.

In concept planting small trays daily is similar to the idea I use in my outdoor garden, with successive plantings over the garden season. With the addition of smaller daily plantings, everything came together and I had a working model for indoor salad gardening.

Ready, Set, Go

With all the pieces of the puzzle in place, it was hard to contain my enthusiasm. Like discovering a star or a planet, I felt this was something new and different for gardeners everywhere. When I would start to tell a friend about it, my kids would groan, "There goes Dad again, talking about the garden!"

But I had a technique that solved the indoor salad garden problem for me, and I knew it would work for others, too. I started to ask gardeners and friends to try my techniques. Some of these folks were novices or friends willing to try just because I asked them to, bless them. Some were experienced gardeners I knew around the country, while others were people I met on gardening websites. Every single gardener who tried them, experienced and novice alike, was excited by the techniques and gave me positive feedback. The unanimous decision was . . . this really works!

I wanted those inexperienced gardeners' reactions, too, to see if the system was simple enough that anyone could do it. My expert gardeners tended to change things and improvise more, so I was interested to see how the technique went over with novices. A friend from Pennsylvania wrote, "I have just one piece of advice for your other trial gardeners: Just follow the instructions!"

The most fun was hearing reactions from kids who tried these techniques and grew their own indoor salad gardens. I still laugh remembering one fourth-grade boy who decided to stage a race between my soil sprouts and a Chia Pet he got for Christmas. In case you're wondering the soil sprouts won hands down.

A Brief History of Sprouts

The history of using young tender shoots as a source of fresh food is murky. A time line would be a guess on my part, so I'll provide a very general idea from the information I could find. But I'll preface this by saying that learning sprout history isn't necessary in order to grow them. My ulterior motive for going back in time was actually to discover more varieties of seeds appropriate for growing shoots today.

A general time line points to the Chinese for the discovery and wide use of sprouting techniques. The first written reference I could find was by Fuxi, Emperor of China in 2852 BC—nearly 5,000 years ago. The Chinese knew they were onto something special—they listed shoots as one of the four great inventions of food, along with bean curd, soy sauce, and gluten. It's reasonable to assume that Chinese immigrants brought their traditional foods and techniques with them to the United States early on, including growing and eating shoots and sprouts. Oddly enough shoots did not find their way into American culture until more recently.

Tracing the popularity of all types of sprouts and shoots these days appears to be a matter of contemporary history. I follow the trail back to Ann Wigmore and Viktoras Kulvinskas working at the Hippocrates Health Institute in Boston, Massachusetts, in the early 1960s. Although their main focus was on the therapeutic use of wheatgrass for health, they also emphasized a raw food diet. One aspect of their regimen was the use of soil-grown sunflower and buckwheat for nutrition. Many a raw-foods teacher, writer, or practitioner credits the influence of these two visionary people and their writings for the introduction of sprouts into our diet today. I join in a tip of the hat to the late Ann Wigmore and to Viktoras Kulvinskas.

For a little over a year, from 1969 to 1970, I worked at the Hippocrates Health Institute myself. One of my jobs was to plant and tend to wheatgrass, sunflower, and buckwheat grown in trays of soil. I also learned to grow alfalfa and mung bean sprouts—at that time we were experimenting with different ways to grow them. The raw food movement focused more on sprouts like alfalfa and mung beans grown in jars, not on soil-grown sprouts. I find growing in soil is a lot easier in the long run and a lot more fun. Among the few drawbacks were the huge trays that made it difficult to do at home, and that problem is no more—it has been solved! Whatever the definitive history of shoots and soil-grown sprouts, I think they're here to stay. We need them not just for the gardening pleasure they offer but as a useful tool to feed ourselves while reducing the resources we use in the process.

Another friend sent pictures of his young son with trays of greens ready to harvest and a big smile on his face. A very nice lady from Kentucky posted her pictures online to display her results!

I was pleased to realize that growing soil sprouts on a windowsill was truly a new and exciting way to enjoy a productive indoor organic garden.

Get ready now to learn the craft of indoor salad gardening. I'll cover every phase of growing in detail in the chapters that follow.

CHAPTER 7

Tools and Accessories

The list of tools you need to grow soil sprouts is short. The first four items on the list—soil, trays, organic fertilizer, and seeds—will be discussed in part II, the how-to section of the book. Most of the rest are items you probably have around the house. Their use will be explained in more detail in the chapters that follow. I'll be brief here to give you a checklist before you get started. For an overview also see the Quick Start Guide on page 49. These are the things you will definitely need:

Soil—standard germination mix
Trays—3-inch by 6-inch (7.6 × 15.2 cm) half-loaf foil baking trays are
    good to start with
Organic fertilizer—manure compost and sea kelp
Seeds—sunflower, pea, radish, buckwheat, and broccoli
Measuring spoons
Measuring cup
Small glass cups or 3-ounce (85.1 g) plastic cups
A small strainer
Scissors
1-gallon (3.8 L) plastic bags
1-gallon (3.8 L) plastic juice container
A warm, dark place
A windowsill
Newspapers or newsprint sheets
Watering can (a plastic soda bottle will work)

These are the things you might want to add to your tool box:

Small cordless vacuum cleaner
A shelf built across the width of a window
Two tubs or boxes to store all the stuff—a seed box and a soil box
Compost bin

The measuring spoons are for the seeds and the fertilizers: A tablespoon, teaspoon, and a half-teaspoon are all that is necessary. The cup is to measure soil and water for the planting medium.

I use small cups to soak the seeds overnight; the 3-ounce (85.1 g) plastic cups work for a teaspoon and tablespoon of seeds, but they are a little tight for 2 tablespoons (29.6 ml) of seeds. You can use the half-pint Mason jar if you want something that will last forever. I use the plastic ones in my classes because they are lightweight and compact. Anything that will hold water will work to soak seeds. Just a tiny word of caution here: Wax-covered cups will not hold water overnight; this was a surprise to me and a lesson learned.

A small strainer about 3 inches (7.6 cm) round, to rinse the seeds after they are soaked, is a must. It should have a fairly fine mesh, particularly if you plan to grow broccoli. Don't be too shocked if the soak water is a little stinky; it is perfectly normal.

Next on the list is scissors. They are for harvest time. I hold a clump of greens in one hand and cut them at the bottom of the stems about

The seed box is a great "tool" for the indoor garden. The seeds are kept dry, and everything needed to start planting is in one place. I don't have enough room in my kitchen to dedicate a whole cupboard for garden supplies, and the box makes it easy to stow everything away in a closet, under the dining table, or, in my case, up in my office!

¼ inch (0.6 cm) above the soil line with the scissors. I have used a knife for this job but find the scissors a lot easier to handle.

One-gallon (3.8 L) plastic bags and 1-gallon (3.8 L) plastic juice containers are for the same purpose, to measure the dry soil mix in preparation for adding water to moisten the mix. I like the juice containers best, but you can see them both in the picture of the soil box.

The warm, dark place and the windowsill and shelves are not tools strictly speaking, but I list them because you need to make them part of your preparations for an indoor garden. I will detail a variety of options for the warm, dark place and the windowsill in chapter 12.

One set of "tools" I want to highlight are the two tubs—I use plastic file boxes. I debated whether these are strictly necessary. They may not be for everyone, but they are indispensable for me. I do all my planting at the kitchen table. I can't keep all my gear, soil, trays, and seeds in the kitchen. There's just not enough room.

So I keep my planting supplies in one tub—the compost, soil, trays, and kelp. I call this one my "dirt box" or the "soil box" sometimes. And I

The soil box has everything needed to plant the soil sprouts. There are 2 gallons (7.6 L) of moistened soil mix ready to plant and 1 gallon (3.8 L) of dry mix ready to refill one of the plastic containers. Also, I keep a small cup of sea kelp meal and a larger container of compost for fertilizer. Measuring spoons and a strainer to rinse the soaked seeds are all you need to start planting.

The seed and soil boxes store under our kitchen table, as shown here, or in some other out-of-the-way place like a closet or back hallway or my office.

use the other tub for the seed-starting supplies—jars of dry seeds, cups for soaking seeds. This one is the "seed box." I keep a set of measuring spoons in both tubs. It's critical to keep the seeds separated from the moist soil to retain the viability of the seeds, so don't use one box for both soil supply and seeds. If I had the extra room in my kitchen, or a room where I could do all my indoor gardening, I might not need these boxes at all, but in a limited-space situation they work great. The tubs are plastic, lightweight, and store neatly in the back hall until I need them. (If company is coming, they go up in my office. If I am really lazy, I'll push them under the kitchen table until my wife notices them.)

One item that may make you scratch your head is the small cordless vacuum cleaner. It's not a big deal. As the sprouts grow a few seeds will drop their rather large hulls onto the windowsill around the tray. I can brush these up with my hand, but I broke down and got a little handheld vacuum to clean up the hulls, and I like it a lot. A dustpan and a broom work just fine, too, but a handheld vacuum is a tool you might like to have and may already own.

You will use a watering can every day. It can be simply a plastic soda bottle or juice jug with a handle or any kind of watering can you happen to have already. For a full shelf of fifteen to twenty small trays, you will need about a half-gallon (236.6 ml) of water. Maybe a little less if it has been cool and cloudy, maybe a little more if the house is warm from a woodstove or heater and it has been a sunny day. Conditions change every day. You will get to know both by the weight of the tray and the dark color of the soil if you need more water or even if you need to skip a day if the tray is very moist. Remember that you can squeeze the soil out like a sponge if you overwater.

Some of the things you do *not* need are grow lights, large expensive shelves, special sprouters, and a window with southern exposure. Equally important, you don't need large quantities of water (it can be a scarce commodity for some) for growing or for cleaning your harvest. This is low-tech, low-impact gardening.

I list a compost bin among the tools because it's important to make provisions for treating leftover soil after cutting your greens. The soil mix

What do all of the watering cans in this picture have in common? They all have spouts. None of them have a sprinkling head or a misting spray. Only use a watering can with a spout so the water goes onto the soil and not on the leaves of the growing greens. The ugly gnome watering can in the picture was a lawn-sale bargain at $2.00; it holds a gallon of water, fits under the kitchen faucet, and has a big spout!

cannot be reused without composting it first. I use a 5-gallon (19 L) bucket during the winter, stuffing it full of used soil and letting it sit outdoors with a lid on it. By spring the soil is ready to use again. The roots that were left behind have decomposed, and the texture is light and friable. The soil has to be fertilized with organic nutrients before you can plant in it again, but since I have a good-sized outdoor garden, I use that composted soil mix for new beds and general sprucing up around the garden, and some of it goes for potting houseplants.

Compost is the heart and soul of any garden and these root-bound cakes of soil left over after the harvest are a great source of green manure and make a rich compost pile. The door at the bottom of this bin opens to give access to the dark finished compost ready to use in the garden indoors or outdoors.

And that's it. All the tools you'll need for an indoor salad garden.

If you're getting excited and want to start gardening—and I assume that a few of you want to plant a tray to see what this is all about—there's a one-page Quick Start Guide coming up on page 49 that will jump-start your gardening experience. If you don't plant right off, the Quick Start Guide is a convenient reference for the future.

For the rest part II is a step-by-step how-to guide with all the details.

How to Grow Soil Sprouts

I teach gardening, and there comes a point in each class when I see smiles and nodding heads and I get the question, "Why haven't I heard about this before?"

When people get it—the idea and how simple it is—they realize they can do this: They can grow a garden indoors. Indoor salad gardening is honest-to-goodness easy. Those moments when I see the light come on for people have special meaning for me. I remember when I first realized the same thing.

Part II covers each element of indoor salad gardening from the ground up. Everything from seed and soil to harvest and salad. And finally I'll run through a typical day of indoor salad gardening to give you a sense of the plant-water-harvest routine. Let's go . . .

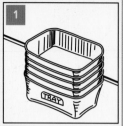

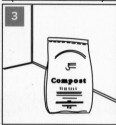

Get Ready Guide
To Plant Five Trays You Will Need:

1. Five 3-inch by 6-inch (7.6 x 15.2 cm) trays (aluminum foil, half-loaf bread pans) or similar, such as five 6-inch (15.2 cm) ceramic cereal bowls
2. 1 gallon (3.8 L) soil mix (standard germination mix), usually peat moss, vermiculite, perlite, and lime
3. 5 tablespoons (74 ml) compost, one per tray (commercial or homemade compost)
4. 3 teaspoons (14.8 ml) liquid sea kelp mixed with water, or 3 teaspoons (14.8 ml) dry kelp meal (use ⅖ teaspoon per tray)
5. 1 tablespoon (14.8 ml) each sunflower, pea, radish, and buckwheat seeds
6. 1 teaspoon (4.9 ml) broccoli seeds (you can substitute Chinese cabbage, kohlrabi, or any Brassica)
7. A stack of newspapers—one full sheet per tray (you can substitute paper towels, newsprint packing paper, or paper napkins)

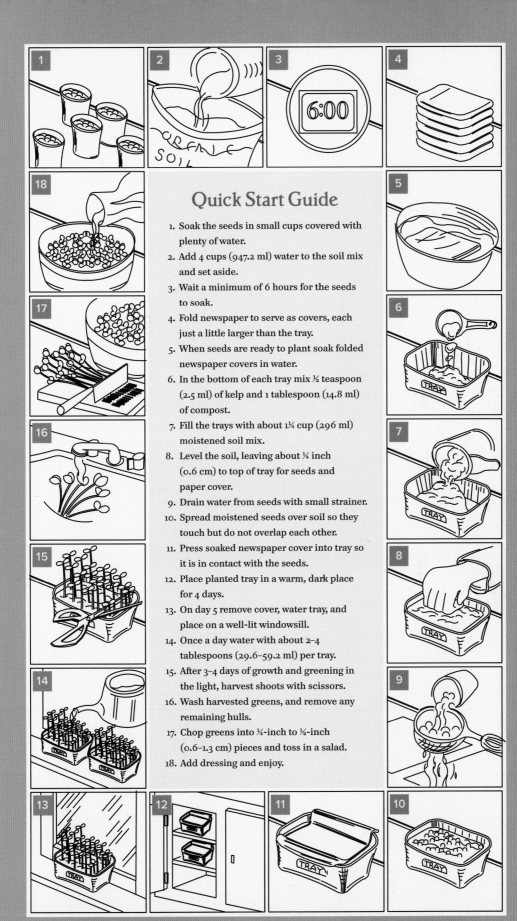

Quick Start Guide

1. Soak the seeds in small cups covered with plenty of water.
2. Add 4 cups (947.2 ml) water to the soil mix and set aside.
3. Wait a minimum of 6 hours for the seeds to soak.
4. Fold newspaper to serve as covers, each just a little larger than the tray.
5. When seeds are ready to plant soak folded newspaper covers in water.
6. In the bottom of each tray mix ⅔ teaspoon (2.5 ml) of kelp and 1 tablespoon (14.8 ml) of compost.
7. Fill the trays with about 1¼ cup (296 ml) moistened soil mix.
8. Level the soil, leaving about ¼ inch (0.6 cm) to top of tray for seeds and paper cover.
9. Drain water from seeds with small strainer.
10. Spread moistened seeds over soil so they touch but do not overlap each other.
11. Press soaked newspaper cover into tray so it is in contact with the seeds.
12. Place planted tray in a warm, dark place for 4 days.
13. On day 5 remove cover, water tray, and place on a well-lit windowsill.
14. Once a day water with about 2–4 tablespoons (29.6–59.2 ml) per tray.
15. After 3–4 days of growth and greening in the light, harvest shoots with scissors.
16. Wash harvested greens, and remove any remaining hulls.
17. Chop greens into ¼-inch to ½-inch (0.6–1.3 cm) pieces and toss in a salad.
18. Add dressing and enjoy.

CHAPTER 8

Seeds

It's hard for me to resist waxing poetic and musing at the miracle that is a seed. For a second each time I start the process of planting, I wonder if it will work one more time. Still, after all these years, the seeds grow like a promise kept.

During class my favorite demonstration is pulling the whole growing mass of sprouts and soil out of a tray to show students the root ball at the bottom of the "soil cake," holding the head of greens in my hands. Growing, alive—and one more time the miracle has happened. Living food for life; it's a poem in 3D.

Seeds Specifically for Sprouting

Seeds for sprouting are different from garden seeds in several ways. First, the sprout seeds don't aim toward a specific result at the end of a long season. Things like color, disease resistance, number of days to harvest, size, shape, and the like are secondary issues. What matters to the indoor salad gardener considering a batch of seeds are things like the germination rate, being free of chemicals, and relatively free of weed seed.

But . . . you can forget about buying bird seed as a way to save money. When I first started experimenting I bought a bag of sunflower seeds and separated the good seed from the sticks, rocks, and broken seeds: I ended up with two piles almost the same size. These seeds are not cleaned, are frequently grown with chemicals, and may be fumigated at the warehouse. And even more ominous, some brands are genetically modified to be infertile so they will not sprout at all!

But help is at hand. Most seed catalogs will specify "seeds for shoots" or something similar. I've included some sources on page 179. My advice is to buy a small quantity at first, try them to see if you like them, *then* buy enough for your indoor salad garden.

I've been surprised more than once by seeds from reputable companies that I routinely plant in my outdoor garden but that don't work for shoots. Being surprised by a pound of seed that doesn't grow well is quite a bit different from having a 50-pound (22.7 kg) bag of seed that's no good. So learn from my experience and try before you buy. Well, try a little before you buy a lot.

Another way to learn something about the seeds you're buying is to ask the order taker if they've ever grown soil sprouts. If they act as if you're speaking a foreign language, proceed with caution.

The Importance of Organic Seed

I've been an organic gardener for a long time. I first subscribed to *Organic Gardening and Farming Magazine* when I was seventeen years old—over 4 decades ago. The option to buy organic has grown exponentially in the past few years, and today there are companies, like my neighbors at High Mowing Organic Seeds, dedicated to offering organic seeds exclusively and to practicing organic farming methods. They're just one of the many farms throughout the United States and Canada that are heroically holding to this standard.

In this age of genetically modified seeds, I'm gratified to see that the demand for standard and heritage varieties has had a rebirth. I hope this demand will outstrip what I consider the reckless experiments of producing genetically modified seeds. For me the last straw is the practice, in order to protect patents, of engineering seed varieties that grow into plants with seeds that are not viable. Described as a "terminator gene," this type of genetic engineering makes me cringe. I could not buy a seed with a "death wish" as part of its internal code. It would take only one mistake by the seed companies to render a wide range of seeds unviable. Thank goodness for organic farmers who are growing viable seeds and maintaining a vital tradition.

A quart jar of larger seeds (sunflower, radish, pea, and buckwheat) is enough to plant one tray every day for 2 months and holds a 6-month supply of the smaller seeds (broccoli, canola, purple kohlrabi).

Should You Consider Commercial Untreated Seeds?

I've used seeds termed "commercial untreated" with good success. Even though they may be produced using conventional farming methods and chemical fertilizers, there's typically no chemical fumigant or treatment used on the seed itself. To my mind these are OK to use for sprouts. I assume that if commercial untreated seeds are not clearly marked "organic," then the seeds are grown with chemical fertilizer, and it is what I am getting for my sprouting seeds. You can make up your own mind on this, but I always choose organic seeds if I can.

Storing Seeds

The goal when storing seeds is to retain their viability for as long as possible. With a few exceptions seeds can be stored for about 2 to 3 years and even up to 5 years. Keeping them dry is the number one priority for retaining viability, so I store all of my seeds in glass or metal containers—canning jars are perfect for the job. A quart jar will hold about a 2-month supply of large seeds and a 6-month supply of the small seeds like broccoli or canola.

The second prerequisite for long-term storage is to keep seeds in a cool climate. Find a spot where the temperature doesn't fluctuate but remains constant and cool. A cold cellar is a good place as long as it isn't damp. An upstairs attic that experiences extremes of hot and cold wouldn't work. A closet on an interior wall has a good chance of keeping a fairly constant temperature without too much fluctuation over several months.

Lastly you do not want to leave seeds in the sunlight for any time at all. Even if you just take the jars out for a few minutes while you're planting, do not leave jars exposed to the sun.

If you have the space, you might consider keeping your seeds in a freezer. Hands down this is the best way to keep them viable and fresh for longer periods. Freezer space is scarce at my place, so I store most of my seeds in canning jars in my office on the north side of the house where there's almost no natural light. Unlike with processed vegetables you can use glass canning jars to store seeds in a freezer because there is no water in the jar to swell and break it. The glass jar will also protect seeds from any moisture buildup inside the freezer. When you're ready to plant let the glass and seeds come to room temperature before you open the jar. That'll prevent condensation from forming on cold seeds and glass surfaces.

Prepare for planting with a tablespoon (14.8 ml) of large seeds for each 3-inch by 6-inch (7.6 × 15.2 cm) tray and only a teaspoon (4.9 ml) of small seeds like the canola seeds pictured here. You can keep a quart jar of each seed in a cupboard for daily plantings. I use my seed box with a 1-quart (946.4 ml) plastic container of each of the large seed types and a 1-cup (236.8 ml) plastic container of each of the small seed types.

Measures

I use two general categories for seeds: large and small.

The large seeds are things like sunflower, radish, buckwheat, and pea. Small seeds are vegetables in the broccoli family, mustard, and others similar in size—smaller than a grain of rice.

For large seeds plant 1 tablespoonful (14.8 ml) in the small 3-inch by 6-inch (7.6 × 15.2 cm) tray. For small seeds plant 1 teaspoonful (4.9 ml) in that same size tray. When I first tried small seeds like broccoli, my initial impulse was to use as much if not more seeds than with larger varieties. It became very clear very quickly that this was a mistake! I only needed one-third the amount of small seed (1 tablespoon = 3 teaspoons) because each tiny seed becomes a full-grown sprout and there are a lot more sprouts in one teaspoon's worth of small seed.

You may have noticed that I refer to volume measurements and not weights here. That's because a tablespoon of sunflower seeds weighs far less than a tablespoon of radish seeds, yet they require the same space when it comes to planting and growing.

Radish seeds pictured here next to their dry seed pods are very easy to grow, harvest, and store. Filling a few gallon jars with seeds for winter greens is akin to having a cold cellar full of garden produce or a woodshed full of firewood; it is a small insurance policy and a good way to keep food costs manageable.

I'll continue discussing seed measures in this way throughout the pages to come. In chapter 15 individual seeds are listed with amounts given. Check these listings for more detailed planting information on specific seeds.

Your Seed Supply

As a rule of thumb 3 to 6 gallons (11.4–22.8 L) of each variety of large seed (like sunflower, pea, radish, and buckwheat) and 1 to 2 gallons (3.8–7.6 L) of each of the small seeds (like broccoli, purple kohlrabi, and canola) constitutes a year's supply if you intend to plant a small tray of each variety every day, with a few large trays for special occasions. Having buckets of seed in the closet is like storing cordwood in the shed, food in the freezer, and rice in the pantry; it's a small insurance policy and a good way to keep food costs manageable.

If you keep an outdoor garden, it's possible to grow plants there specifically to harvest seeds for shoots, and it's not difficult. Or should I say *some* of the seeds are easy to grow.

Most of the larger seeds like sunflower, pea, and even radish are not difficult for the average gardener to manage and harvest. The broccoli family needs two seasons to produce seeds, so I've ruled out growing my own for sprouting, at least for now.

Radishes were something new for me. The first time I tried growing them for seed, I was surprised by the shape of the pods; they looked like hot peppers. Being the curious type I nibbled on a few pods and found they were delicious when still in the immature stage. I thought I had discovered something novel when, lo and behold, I found out that radishes have been grown in India just for their pods—a variety called Rat-Tail radish—for many years.

Growing your own seeds is not only rewarding and economical, but you don't have to worry about cross-pollination occurring because you're only growing until you get shoots. The plant seed itself doesn't have to be true to type, which is required for commercial growing. There isn't room here to go into detailed techniques—that will have to be the subject of another book—but if you're an adventurous gardener growing plants for seed is fun to try, and it's particularly satisfying to glean a year's supply of seeds from your own garden.

Fresh radish pods swell around the seeds as they form, sort of like a bean or pea pod. Let them dry on the vine, then harvest, and continue to dry in a covered airy spot like a porch. That is, of course, if you don't eat them first!

CHAPTER 9
Soil versus a Soil-Less Growing Medium

I know it may seem confusing, but the soil I refer to for growing soil sprouts is really a growing medium made up of peat moss, vermiculite, and perlite and not soil like dirt from a garden. This is a key factor to success, and I want to emphasize that you should not use bagged topsoil or commercial compost either—use only a standard germination mix.

A General Explanation of Soil Mixes

Growing soil sprouts is much like growing houseplants in containers or growing vegetables in self-watering pots outdoors. I think of it as "container gardening lite" or minicontainer gardening.

The best medium to use indoors is a soil-less mix, so-called because it's composed primarily of peat moss, vermiculite, and perlite, with no actual soil—that is, there's no actual dirt like you have in your garden in the mix. There's usually some limestone included in a soil-less mix (also called a germination mix), and that's perfectly fine for sprouts.

The characteristics of the growing medium that I recommend for soil sprouts are: good water retention, light and friable texture, and sterility. This doesn't mean sterile like in an operating room, just that there's no dirt in it that might carry fungus or organisms that promote mold growth.

Most potting soil or germination mixes work fine. The things you *do not* want in your potting mix are any hydro-gels (silicone pellets) that retain water in a container. Those are meant for flower pots and should *not* be used for growing food. Also stay away from the mixes that contain chemical fertilizers, whether slow-release or otherwise. I add my own organic fertilizers at the time of planting.

One more note: Several of these mixes contain what is known as an endomycorrhizal inoculant. Mycorrhizal fungi establish a beneficial relationship with plant roots, and although they're more important when growing sets, they're fine for soil sprouts, too. They're approved for organic gardens by the Organic Materials Review Institute (OMRI), so it's OK to use these mixes.

For the sake of economy you can buy potting mix at the garden shop in so-called 3.9 bales (bale sizes typically range from 3.7 to 3.9 cubic feet [.11 cubic meters]). Smaller 2.2 bales are also handy, depending on your situation—how much room you have to store the bale and how easily you can handle an awkward, heavy bale. Sometimes the smaller one is worth the extra expense.

You can also pick up mixes in 20-quart (18.9 L) or 60-quart (56.8 L) bags, and if you're starting small, these will work fine. Be careful not to buy straight peat moss, which looks similar in packaging but doesn't work as well as a growing medium for soil sprouts because the vermiculite holds more water and provides the light texture we need for the tiny roots.

You will need a germination mix to get ready to plant your indoor salad garden. I measure the dry soil mix into 1-gallon (3.8 L) containers for easy storage in the soil box. They are ready to add 4 cups (947.2 ml) of water to when needed for planting. Besides a few bags of dry soil mix, I usually keep two or three premoistened bags of soil mix for planting. Once the soil mix is moistened you will not need to add any water until the trays are set out into the light.

Premeasuring Your Soil

Once I have my bag or bale of potting soil at home, I like to repackage it into 1-gallon (3.8 L) plastic bags. It's easier to store that way, and premeasuring makes the routine of daily planting easier to organize. It may seem like an unnecessary effort, but it comes in handy when watering. The proportion of water to potting mix is key to a proper sprouting recipe, and too much or too little moisture in the soil can cause problems. Premeasuring the soil and adding 4 cups (947.2 ml) of water to the bag makes a perfect planting mix every time.

A 1-gallon (3.8 L) plastic juice container with a handle makes a great scoop for the soil mix. It is a

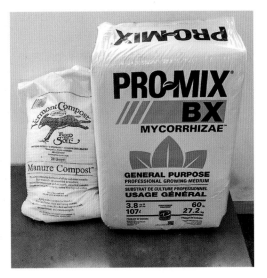

Make sure you get a mix of peat moss, vermiculite, and perlite, not just peat moss alone. Some have added limestone and that is OK, but don't buy a mix that has added fertilizer or anything to retain moisture. These are usually chemicals, and we don't want them and don't need them for indoor gardening. Any compost will work, but this brand, available to me locally, is a premium mix of organic materials.

fine tool to transfer soil from bale to bags. The bale of soil mix arrives hard and packed tight, so break it up first with a garden trowel. Dumping the bale into a clean 30-gallon (28.4 L) garbage pail can make it easier to break up, too, and then scoop the soil into gallon bags.

Plan to end up with about fifty gallon bags of soil from one 3.9 bale. Each gallon bag will fill from ten to twelve small trays for planting. I plant four or five trays each day for my family of four. One 3.9 bale lasts me about one hundred days, so I use about three or four bales a year.

Avoid Using Your Garden Soil

Veteran gardeners attending my workshops frequently ask: "Can I use the good soil from my garden or compost pile for an indoor garden?"

The short answer is no. Not without a little preparation.

There are good reasons to avoid garden soil. One simple mechanical reason is that soil is hard for the sprout roots to penetrate. Although it seems light and friable, even excellent garden soil develops a crust that's difficult for the new roots to penetrate. Remember you're "planting" the sprout seeds *on top of* the soil. The roots have to dig down for themselves.

The fuzzy stuff at the bottom of the stems on these sunflowers is just root hair and *not* mold. The most frequent question I get is identifying mold. The next picture makes it crystal clear what mold looks like.

An equally important reason not to use garden soil is the added risk of damp off and mold. Garden soil and most homemade composts are rich with molds and bacteria. For the outdoor garden these are good. But they cause problems indoors where dark, moist conditions create the perfect environment for damp off, which can quickly kill your soil sprouts. Damp off isn't a problem when you use a peat-vermiculite mix.

You may have exceptional outdoor soil with lots of peat moss or sand in it, and I see no reason not to try using it, but you should sterilize it first, and that takes some work. You must first let the soil dry out, and then "sterilize" it in a solar cooker or an oven.

I suggest that you begin by growing soil sprouts in a commercial germination mix, learning the ropes of indoor salad gardening first, before experimenting with your own soils. That way you'll have a standard by which to measure your results with the outdoor soil.

Making Your Own Germination Mix

For the adventurous gardener the following is a recipe for making 4 gallons (15.2 L) of your own germination mix:

3 gallons (11.4 L) peat moss
½ gallon (1.9 L) vermiculite

This is mold; it has a hairy look, but the most distinct characteristic is the brown stem and the fact that the plants are dying. If you get mold, the whole tray will likely die off, so you will have to start over with a new batch. This is almost always a result of using dirt alone.

½ gallon (1.9 L) perlite
¼ cup (59.2 ml) limestone

Place ingredients in a wheelbarrow or on a tarp, and mix thoroughly with a trowel or hoe. Fill 1-gallon (3.8 L) bags with the finished mix and seal to keep dry. When you're getting ready to plant your garden, add 4 cups (947.2 ml) water to each bag and reseal the bags to moisturize the soil mix.

The recipe above will almost fill a 5-gallon (19 L) bucket. If you expect to plant a large number of trays at one time, you might do better to store the whole bucket, moistened with 14 cups (3.3 L) of water and covered to let it soak.

Making your own germination mix is pretty easy to do, and it makes sense if you already have the ingredients in your garden shed, you have the room to do it where making a mess won't matter to anyone, and—like me—you just plain old enjoy doing this kind of gardening project.

Considering Coir (Shredded Coconut Fiber)

Coir is gaining popularity as a biodegradable and environmentally sound renewable substitute for peat moss (it is pronounced like the word core), but I've had mixed results in my experiments with it.

The product is composed of ground-up hulls of coconuts. It's really remarkable stuff. I purchased coir in compressed 2-inch (5.1-cm) round tablets, put one in a tray, added water and, presto, the tray was full of dirt in minutes. It's amazing to watch. When soaked in hot water the material swells to eight times its original size.

But I'm not sold on it for all my soil sprouts. Some greens grow as well in coir as in the peat germination mix, some do not. I still add fertilizers, just as I do with my regular mix, and have even tried adding a trace of lime to make the coir less acidic. But on the whole I've found the peat mix is cheaper and more reliable. But if you have a ready supply of coir, it works well enough, so go ahead and use it.

Coir also comes in bricks that measure about 8 inches by 4 inches by 2 inches (20.3 × 10.2 × 5.1 cm), which I find a little more difficult to work with. I've sawn off a slice like cutting a loaf of bread and cut the slice into 2-inch by 2-inch (5.1 × 5.1 cm) chunks for use in a 3-inch by 6-inch (7.6 ×

Coir comes in big tablets or bricks and is easy to reconstitute into soil. I put a chunk in a tray along with the compost and sea kelp and then add lots of water. The tray on the left only took a few minutes to turn into moist soil. It is a good idea to mix it with vermiculite and a little lime to make it a germination mix.

15.2 cm) tray. Three bricks of coir make the equivalent of 1 cubic foot (.11 cubic meters) of peat moss, enough to fill nearly forty small trays.

This stuff is just plain fun to watch expand. Young kids get a real kick out of it. If you plan to use coir, though, I suggest that you moisten three bricks and mix this with ½ gallon (3.8 L) each of vermiculite and perlite, with ¼ cup (59.2 ml) of granular limestone. Combine all the ingredients together, and bag the entire mix until planting time. The mix can be stored like this for months, but I usually keep two or three bags of moistened soil ready for planting.

Coir is on the National Organic Program (NOP) List of Allowed Substances. It also carries the distinguished commendation of the Wildlife Conservation Society as an ecologically sustainable product that supports good conservation.

Using Just Perlite

I've tried using perlite alone in my trays. I thought that if it works for hydroponics it might be good for soil sprouts, but for some reason it's not. The roots of the greens don't penetrate well and they grow more slowly. Also, the roots don't hold the plant steady and they tend to tip easily. During my experiments I realized that I'd also have a harder time recycling a large quantity of perlite to my outdoor garden. My conclusion: The germination mix has worked fine for a long time running. It's still the best choice, in my view.

I tend to be kind of fussy about my gardening. As a matter of fact I like things to work *perfectly*. I'll experiment with different techniques until I get things just right.

The Importance of the Water to Dry Soil Ratio: Stick to the Formula

When I first started indoor salad gardening, I had worked out the proportions of water to germination mix using gallon bags for measuring and mixing soil and water. At one point I ran out of bags and thought I'd try scooping the dry soil mix out of the mixing barrel into trays, then adding water right in the individual trays. It was tough to judge just how much water to add to each single tray and even harder to be patient while the soil absorbed the water. I kept adding a little more water, then a little more, and the next thing I knew I had a tray full of mud. Soggy soil is no good for sprouts.

So, I tried pouring off the extra water and compressing the soil to dry it out even more. It didn't work, but I was bullheaded about making this routine do the job, and I stuck with it for a few weeks. Then I came across a couple of old gallon bags of soil that had been stored up in my office. I added a measured amount of water, sealed them up again, and went to soak some seeds. The next morning I opened the bag of soil mix to fill the trays, and the soil mix was, ahem, perfect. It was moist but still loose and friable, and planting was easy and simple, just the way I like it.

I had to laugh at myself. I'd put so much time into figuring out the very best mix and the easiest routine for planting soil sprouts, and then I ignored it all in a stubborn attempt to perfect a completely different method. It was gratifying to come full circle and admit that individual gallon bags of soil mix work best. Dare I say they work perfectly!

I bring this up now to emphasize the importance of maintaining the proportion of water to dry mix as 4 cups (947.2 ml) water to 1 gallon (3.8 L) dry soil mix—whether the soil is store-bought or homemade. As part of your indoor garden it is handy to have several gallon containers of moistened soil ready to plant the next batch of soaked seeds.

In the last two chapters we have gone over seeds and now soil for planting, so next let's look at what to plant in—the various options for garden trays and planters.

CHAPTER 10
Trays and Planters

When I first started growing soil sprouts, I tried out a bunch of different trays. I found that just about anything that holds soil and water works fine. I tell the students in my workshop classes that the contents of a recycle bin are a treasure trove of great containers for sprouting.

A Wide Variety of Possibilities

You need something that holds about an inch and a half of soil for the minimum depth. And a tray 3 or 4 inches (7.6 or 10.2 cm) wide fits nicely on just about any windowsill. The idea is to figure out *where* you plan to put your trays before you decide *what* trays to use.

After one of my classes I met a student at our local farm store. She was busy with a pen and paper when I saw her in the aisle. She explained that a 12-inch (30.5 cm) saucer—the kind typically placed under a red clay pot—had almost the same volume as five of the small trays that I had suggested for indoor gardens. She had figured that out standing there, pen and paper in hand. It turned out she had a huge bay window where she planned to green her sprouts, so there was plenty of room for these huge trays. I was so pleased that I bought one to try!

There's no one-size-fits-all (nor one-shape-fits-all) for this. Home design varies considerably; you may have a bay window where you plan to green your sprouts, or you may have only narrow windowsills on all your windows. You may be planning to build a shelf just for indoor salad gardening, or you may have a shelf already in use for houseplants that will share space with your sprout trays. All of the possibilities around your house or apartment mean you can choose from a wide variety of trays. That's one of the advantages of this technique—it's flexible.

It's fun to see how each person takes the basics and then personalizes an indoor salad garden. I've even planted soil sprouts to use as centerpieces at our local food cooperative's annual meeting using ceramic ovals that I found at a dollar store. They were just the right size to fit on the windowsills while they were growing, and they looked really pretty on the tables.

Table 10.1. Trays by the Square Inch

Tray Size	Sq. In.	Large Seed	Small Seed	Compost	Kelp	Soil
		Tbsp.	Tsp.	Tbsp.	Tsp.	Cup
3″ × 6″	18	1	1	1	½	1½
4″ × 8″	32	2	2	2	1	2½
6″ × 8″	48	3	3	3	1½	4
10″ × 10″	100	5	5	5	2½	9
4″ Circle	13	1	1	1	½	1
5″ Circle	20	1	1	1	½	1½
6″ Circle	28	2	2	2	1	2
10″ Circle	80	4	4	4	2	9

The possibilities are endless, so have fun finding trays that work for you. I enjoy poking around at thrift stores or yard sales with an eye for a great tray. Just be sure the pot or ceramic bowl is appropriate for growing plants for food. I suppose I should point out that any type of lead, pewter, or soldered metal should never be used as a planter. And for plastic I only use agricultural grade trays like the kind used for garden sets and starts. If in doubt about the material the tray is made of, don't use it.

Clay Pots, Cedar Boxes, and Pressed Peat Pots

Nurseries and farm stores carry many interesting clay pots that work well for planting, but they can be pricey, so remember when you're shopping that all you really need is a cheap old foil bread pan. That might temper the urge to get another pretty pot.

I happen to like the cedar boxes I get from the Fedco catalog (Fedco is a garden supply cooperative in Maine). The boxes work well, and they're a local and renewable product here in New England, but you need to line the interior with paper to keep soil and water from slipping out between the cracks. They only come in one size—about the same area as a large tray (4 inches × 8 inches [10.2 × 20.3 cm])—so plan your quantities accordingly. A little creative work in a woodshop can produce about the same thing if you have access to cedar boards. In fact most types of wood are safe to grow soil sprouts in as long as they're untreated—definitely do not use weatherized or pressure-treated woods.

Another option is to use pressed peat planters. They'll last through five planting cycles, then begin to degrade. They're available in fairly small sizes to suit your harvest needs. You'll want to put a tray of some sort under them, though; they tend to absorb moisture, and it collects underneath the planter—not good for the wood finish on your windowsill.

My Choice of Tray

The trays I prefer, for both my family garden and my commercial garden, are aluminum foil bread pans. The 1-pound (453.6 g) half-loaf size and the 2-pound (907.2 g) whole-loaf pans are inexpensive, durable, and I can reuse them for months before recycling them. The half-loaf pan measures 3 inches by 6 inches (7.6 × 15.2 cm), and it's about 2 inches (5.1 cm) deep—I refer to this as the small tray. The large tray is a whole-loaf pan that measure 4 inches by 8 inches by 2 inches deep (10.2 × 20.3 × 5.1 cm). I've had good results with these trays, and so I recommend that my students start with them until they have the technique down pat. After that they can experiment with other choices, but it's easier to judge results if they've already had some success with one technique first.

I had an e-mail conversation with a fellow who worked for a large commercial grower of sprouts in Massachusetts. The company grew greens on trays that were measured in feet, not inches, so when he read on my website that for 2 months of sprouts I used 3½ cups (828.8 ml) of seeds to plant 3-inch by 6-inch (7.6 × 15.2 cm) trays, he thought I meant

To get ready to plant your indoor salad garden, you will need trays. My personal favorites are the foil loaf pans. The small tray, a half-loaf pan, is 3 inches wide by 6 inches long by 2 inches deep (7.6 × 15.2 × 5.1 cm). The larger trays on the left are 4 inches by 8 inches by 2 inches (10.2 × 20.3 × 5.1 cm). I suggest starting with the small trays until you're comfortable with the technique. A simple ceramic cereal bowl is another good choice, and it is kind of nice to throw them in the dishwasher after each use.

a 3-foot by 6-foot (91.4 × 182.9 cm) area! "There's no way," he said. "That's just not enough seeds."

When I explained that I was using 3 *inch* × 6 *inch* containers, planting a little every day just for my family's salad bowl, he had a tough time visualizing such small amounts.

The telling part of the conversation was when he confessed that he didn't grow any greens for himself. Because he planted on such a large scale at work, the thought of growing greens at home seemed implausible. When the light came on and he realized he could grow his own greens right there in his apartment, he was a happy guy. "It is so simple, I don't know why I didn't think of it."

Size to Fit Your Harvest Needs

Besides fitting on a windowsill the small trays provide the amount I need to harvest on a daily basis. I plant five of these trays every day—one each of sunflower, radish, buckwheat, pea, and broccoli—to meet our salad needs, about 12 to 16 ounces (340.2 × 453.6 g) of greens for my family of four. This makes for a nice variety of textures, flavors, colors, and nutrients in one salad.

If you have a larger contingent of salad eaters on your hands, you can approach a larger harvest in two ways: plant more small trays or move up to the larger trays (4 inch by 8 inch [10.2 × 20.3 cm]). At one point when one of my sons was home for the summer, he wanted more sunflower greens, so I planted one large tray of those every day along with the usual small trays of radish, pea, buckwheat, and broccoli. It was a functional, easy adjustment to my planting routine.

I personally like pea shoots for use in a stir-fry vegetable dish I make once or twice a week, so I plant a couple of large trays of peas every week to fill that harvest need, too. These trays sit on a set of shelves I installed in our TV room right next to the stationary bike we use for exercise. They give me extra oxygen, and I give them carbon dioxide in return.

The point is, when you're sizing up your trays, size up the harvest as well. Fit the tray to your own need for greens. That's a principle I learned to apply outdoors in my earth garden; it's the same for an indoor salad garden.

CHAPTER 11

Fertilizer

The soil mix containing peat moss, vermiculite, and perlite is an excellent base as a growing medium, but it has little nutrition for the soil sprouts. Not that the greens need much because there is a store of nutrition in the seed itself, but my experience has shown that small amounts of fertilizer added to the trays make for lush growth in each planting cycle, and the shoots stay green for a few days longer in the tray.

Compost

Compost is the miracle worker of gardening. Tests have shown that as little as ⅛ inch (1.9 ml) of compost on the garden is beneficial for the plants (see *Organic Gardening* [OG], Spring 2007 page 21). I would not—could not—recommend any type of chemical fertilizer for the indoor salad garden. Compost does the job perfectly.

I add 1 tablespoon (14.8 ml) of compost and ½ teaspoon (2.5 ml) of sea kelp to the bottom of each small tray (twice that amount for the large

A tablespoon of compost in each small tray is enough to fertilize the fast-growing soil sprouts. I buy a 6- or 20-quart (5.7 L or 18.9 L) bag and transfer 3 cups (710.4 ml) into a plastic container to keep handy in my soil box.

The root mass at the bottom of the tray is so tightly packed in the soil that it forms a "soil cake" that goes to the compost pile after each harvest. When I first noticed this I realized that the compost and sea kelp belonged at the bottom of the tray.

trays). Looking at the root system that develops after only 7 days, you'll see why I put the fertilizer in first at the bottom of the tray. This is what I meant back in chapter 8 when I described removing the soil cake from a tray to show my classes what the bottom looks like. That's where the roots congregate to form a massive root ball. Putting the fertilizer where the roots collect assures every opportunity for the fast-growing shoots to get the nutrients they need.

The compost I use comes from a local producer, Vermont Compost Company in Montpelier, Vermont. It's a well-designed organic mix based on biodynamic principles, with greensand and granite dust, several types of manure, and other organic materials like mash from a local apple cider press. It's a splendid resource right next door to where I live. But lots of compost mixes are available through most garden supply stores and catalogs, and any organic compost will work to fertilize your soil sprouts.

Even your own homegrown compost can do the job, though homegrown compost has a few drawbacks.

For instance your own compost may still have some earthworms in it, and while some would argue that having earthworms in your trays isn't a drawback, the worms may not stay in the container and may decide to wander. There's also a chance that you'll find fruit flies or other critters spawning in your trays. Again some may not consider these to be problems, but I do.

To prevent critter problems I recommend you "sterilize" homemade compost and bag it.

Sterilizing Your Own

I guess what I mean is more like dehydrating the compost than sterilizing it. On a hot, sunny summer day spread your compost in shallow trays outdoors and let it dry completely. To test it take a handful of the compost and squeeze. If it holds together, it needs another day or two in the sun. When it is dry and crumbles, bag it for use later. And remember to bag up enough to make it through the winter if you live in the colder climes. It'll be tough to break into a frozen compost pile if you run out.

To know how much you'll need, a little math will help here: If you plant five trays a day, that's 5 tablespoons (74 ml) of compost a day (one for each tray), or about 150 tablespoons (2.2 L) (30 days by 5 tablespoons [74 ml]) a month. That's a little more than half a gallon of compost every month. A year's supply for me would be about 6 or 7 gallons (22.8 or 26.6 L). Do your own math, and make sure to dry enough to get you through the winter.

Kelp Meal and Liquid Seaweed

In addition to compost I use either a liquid seaweed or a dry kelp meal for the trace minerals and additional nitrogen my sprouts need. Dry kelp meal is easier to handle and store, but I've come to prefer the liquid seaweed. Either one does the job, placed in the bottom of the tray before it is filled with soil mix.

Sea kelp makes a large number of trace minerals available to the sprouts. I think of it as growing my own vitamin pills! The kelp is also a growth enhancer, helping seedlings to absorb other nutrients, which in turn makes them available to my family in a salad. How it works may not be completely understood, but it's well

Use ½ teaspoon (2.5 ml) of either liquid seaweed or dry kelp meal. I soak the dry kelp meal in about a tablespoon (4.9 ml) of water to reconstitute the kelp and make the nutrients more available to the roots. Although the seaweed is considered a fertilizer, it is most notably a "growth enhancer" for seedlings. I have observed that the leaves stay greener in the trays longer, and that's enough reason for me!

accepted empirically that sea kelp meal gives young shoots a boost. I've compared growing soil sprouts with and without, and my own experience tells me it's well worth the cost and effort to add kelp.

Worm Castings

I've had students in my workshops who cultivate their own worm castings for fertilizer. They use vermiculture (worm composting) to compost their kitchen waste and have plenty available. Some of these folks have generously given me bags of worm castings for my test gardens, and the castings work well as a fertilizer. The same instructions apply when using your own worm castings as when using your own compost, detailed above. That is, the castings need to be dried and stored for later use.

Use the worm castings as you do compost and sea kelp: Put a small amount at the bottom of the tray before the soil mix goes into the tray.

CHAPTER 12
Planting, Growing, and Greening

Now that you understand the principles that form the foundation for soil sprout gardening and you've gathered the necessary equipment and resources, you're ready to get to work.

Soaking the Seeds

The first step in planting your soil sprouts is soaking the seeds in water. Place a tablespoon of seeds in a small plastic or glass cup, fill it with fresh water, and let them soak for a minimum of 6 hours but not more

Now that we are ready to start, the first step is to soak the seeds for at least 6 and up to 24 hours. This picture shows my daily planting of one small tray each of sunflower, buckwheat, canola, radish, and peas. The harvest from this planting will be about 12 to 16 ounces (340.2–453.6 g) of fresh greens.

than 24 hours. Use one container (cup) for each tray with one type of seed in it. Some seeds, like sunflower or buckwheat, will float at first until they soak up enough water to sink into the water. I push them down to help them get wet.

The cups don't have to be kept in the dark, but it's a good idea to keep them out of direct sunlight. Sprout seeds are very forgiving; if you soak them at night—which is what I usually do—and cannot plant the next morning, you can put off planting until that evening.

When I have the seeds all soaked and ready but I run into a time crunch and can't plant right away (that is, within the 24-hour window), I let them begin to sprout right in the cup, then plant them as soon as possible. Rinse and drain the water off, and just keep the seeds in their cups for planting the next day. I have let them go even longer than this—they had roots about a half inch long—and still planted and harvested a crop.

Some Things Are Flexible, Some Are Not

You'll notice throughout these instructions that I let you know what leeway you have, just in case. With kids in school, long work hours, teaching workshops, writing a book, and all the rest to be done, I've had to learn how to stretch things out and make indoor salad gardening work around *my* schedule. The question of just how long I can actually put off planting those soaked seeds has come up more than once. It's important to know which instructions are flexible and which ones should be followed to the letter. In this case you have some flexibility for soaking and planting your seeds after 6 hours, but 6 hours is the minimum soak time for the seeds to start germination. And that's consistent with all the varieties.

The Soak Process

I use all sorts of cups to soak the seeds. Anything that holds water will work. For 1 to 2 tablespoons (14.8 ml–29.6 ml) of seeds at a time, the smallest Ball or Mason jars do the job. For my workshops I use the little 3-ounce (85 g) plastic Solo cups because they're small and easy to transport. Sometimes a 9-ounce (255.2 g) plastic cup is called for when I am getting ready to plant a batch of large trays. Plastic cups are easy to work with in quantity and are reusable. If you choose paper cups, make sure to use a tray underneath them because they frequently leak.

To soak, measure seeds into the cups and fill with water to a level at least ½ inch (1.3 cm) above the seeds. In this case too much water is better than too little. It's important for the seeds to absorb as much water as they want. Peas will soak up a lot, so make sure they have plenty. A guideline is: Maintain a ratio of 1 tablespoon (14.8 ml) of seeds to at least 2 tablespoons (29.6 ml) of water.

Prepare the Soil

To prepare your soil mix pour 3½ to 4 cups (828.8–947.2 ml) of water into 1 gallon (3.8 L) of dry mix. I use either a 1-gallon plastic bag or a 1-gallon plastic juice container for this job. Let me emphasize: Measure carefully because too much or too little moisture will cause trouble for your seeds during their 4-day incubation period. As I mentioned earlier I'll let you know which rules you can stretch, and this one you should follow carefully.

Just in case check to be sure you have enough moistened soil mix at about the same time as you soak the seeds. If you need to prepare more at that point, the water will be absorbed into the peat moss evenly by the time you want to use it. I keep two bags of moist soil mix ready in my dirt box so I can plant a batch of five trays without stopping to mix up more. If you have the space to store it, it's fine to keep a number of bags pre-moistened; they'll be good for months as long as the bags are sealed. If you're ready to plant and you forgot to mix soil with water, you have a couple of remedies.

- Use a tall, narrow, 1-gallon (3.8 L) juice container and hot water. Fill the container with dry soil and pour the hot water in. The narrow shape of the container distributes the water and moistens the soil more quickly.
- Put the soil mix into a large mixing bowl and pour water over it. Knead it thoroughly by hand to moisten the peat evenly. (If you don't want very dirty hands, wear rubber gloves for this job.)

This last option can be accomplished by kneading the material right in a plastic bag, too, so you don't have to put your hands into the dirt. Any light brown peat lets

Pour 3½ to 4 cups (828.8–947.2 ml) of water into 1 gallon (3.8 L) of soil mix and let it sit for a while, about 20 minutes minimum, to give the mix a chance to absorb the water evenly. If you are in a hurry, pour the soil and the water into a bowl and knead roughly for a few minutes so you can use the moistened mix right away.

you know that it's not ready yet, so keep kneading until the soil is dark and moist throughout.

A note on logistics and multi-tasking: This is the time to fold your paper covers and get them soaking so they're ready to go on when the seeds are planted.

Paper Covers

Any kind of newsprint, newspaper, paper towels, paper napkins—all of these "pulp" papers are good for covers. You should make sure you have enough on hand when you start to plant. Presoak them until they're fully saturated. Napkins and paper towels only need a

When the seeds have soaked and you're ready to plant, take a stack of newspapers and fold them to fit the trays you are using. For example, I fold a single large sheet in half, then in half again, then into thirds so I end up with twelve layers of newsprint about 4 inches wide by 7 inches long (10.2 × 17.8 cm). A double sheet of a paper towel will work just as well as the newsprint. Don't worry about stacking up too many layers of paper on the seeds; the tiny shoots can handle a lot of weight, and as the covers dry out they lighten up quite a bit.

quick dip in the water to be ready, but newsprint will need about a 10-minute soak to take up enough water. Try this—pull a newsprint cover out of the bowl of water after soaking for only a minute. You can feel what I mean; it's still lightweight, not much heavier than dry paper. If you have

Place the paper covers in a bowl of water, and let them soak while you get the trays ready and plant the seeds. They need about 10 minutes to soak, but longer is OK; they will feel heavy when the paper is saturated. Usually this initial soaking will keep the paper moist for the first 4 days in the dark.

a roll of newsprint (usually 24 inches [61 cm] wide), tear off a 12-inch-wide (30.5 cm) strip of paper and fold it in half lengthwise, then in half one more time, then fold it in thirds to make a pad of paper about 4 inches wide and 7 inches long (10.2 × 17.8 cm). When the paper is sopping wet you can easily push it into the tray and form fit it, so if it is a little big that is fine. But do push it into the tray so the wet paper makes firm contact with the seeds. If you are using a sheet of newspaper, it's the same idea—fold the paper in such a way that it fits the tray with a little extra all around.

If for some reason you don't have paper to use, certainly scraps of cloth could be used as well, you just have to experiment a little with the right combination of layers that works for the material you are using.

Fill the Tray with Growing Medium

Place your fertilizers in the bottom of your tray: 1 tablespoon (14.8 ml) of compost and ½ teaspoon (2.5 ml) of sea kelp meal or liquid sea kelp for each small tray.

My students frequently ask, "Why don't you mix the fertilizer with the soil mix?" As I mentioned previously sprout roots grow to the bottom of the tray and form a mass there—a root ball. They don't grow back up into the soil mix, as you might think, so I put the fertilizer at the bottom of the tray where that mass of roots can absorb it. The peat just holds a reserve of water for the plants as they grow.

When ready to start planting, 1 tablespoon (14.8 ml) of compost and ½ teaspoon (2.5 ml) of kelp meal goes at the bottom of the small tray. The roots ball up in the bottom of the tray, so that is the best place to put the compost and sea kelp.

Fill the tray with moistened soil mix. The small tray will need about 1¼ cups (296 ml), but do not fill the tray to the brim. Leave about ¼ inch (0.6 cm) space at the top for the seeds and the daily watering.

You can observe this yourself. After you harvest the greens take the soil cake out of the tray and break it open. You'll see how the sprout roots extend directly down to the bottom of the tray and then grow in circles around the edges. I have never seen roots grow back up into the soil mix. Given enough time perhaps they would, but in their short growing season they form a mat of roots at the bottom of the soil.

After the fertilizers, sea kelp, and compost are placed in the bottom of your tray, put about 1¼ cups (296 ml) of moistened soil mix into a small tray and level it off but don't press it down. The soil should be nice and fluffy for the roots to grow down easily. Remove any sticks and break up clumps on the surface for the same reason. Leave about ¼ inch (0.6 cm) of space at the top of the container for the paper cover you'll install during the first stage and to hold water in the second stage of growth. If you fill to the top of the tray, the seeds along the edge tend to dry out, and water easily spills over before it can be soaked up by the soil.

Now your tray is ready for seeds. Note that if you're planting a different-sized tray than the small 3 inch by 6 inch (7.6 × 15.2 cm), the proportions should stay the same. For instance my large tray (4 inch by 8 inch [10.2 × 20.3 cm]) is almost twice the area of my small tray (32 square inches versus 18 square inches [207.1 vs. 412.1 cm²]), so I use 2

With your fingers level off the soil so it is about ¼ inch (0.6 cm) down from the top of the tray rim. It is important to have a little room for the water to puddle before it is absorbed into the soil. I am not saying to pack the soil down, just level it off to make an even surface to spread out the seeds.

tablespoons (29.6 ml) of compost and 1 teaspoon (4.9 ml) of sea kelp to about 2⅓ cups (592 ml) of soil mix. Whatever size tray it's easy to calculate the proportions of fertilizer and soil, starting with the basic ratios of 1¼ cup (296 ml) soil to ½ teaspoon (2.5 ml) kelp meal or liquid kelp and 1 tablespoon (14.8 ml) of compost. Approximate measures are fine; exact ratios are not critical here.

"Plant" the Seeds

Next, as we learned earlier, you won't actually plant the seed in the normal way under the soil. You're going to spread seeds out on top of the soil.

First drain the water off of the soaking seeds, give them a quick rinse in fresh water to remove any dirt from the seed hulls, and then drain them again. It's worth noting that the soak-water tends to

Rinse the soaked seeds in fresh water before planting them. I pour the seeds into a small strainer and give them a quick rinse at the faucet and then dump them right into the prepared tray.

ferment a little, so I like to make sure I rinse well with fresh water to lower the risk of damp off or the seeds rotting.

Then place the rinsed seeds right on top of the soil. With your fingers spread the seeds out over the soil—they'll touch each other, but they shouldn't overlap. For smaller seeds like broccoli you can use a spoon to spread them out. (I call it "spooncasting" rather than broadcasting the seeds.) Use the entire area of the tray; seeds can even touch the sides of the tray.

Place the seeds right on top of the soil, and spread them out evenly so they touch but don't overlap each other. For small seeds like broccoli you might find it easier to use the back of a spoon to spread the seeds.

With your fingers or knuckles press the seeds down gently but firmly so they make good contact with the moist soil. They need to survive the next 4 days on this moisture—we will not water them again until after the cover comes off. (See chapter 15 for detailed planting instructions for each seed variety.)

Cover the Tray

Paper covers are the trick that lets us plant on top of the soil. The covers replace dirt in an outdoor garden that normally keeps seeds moist and dark until they sprout.

When the paper is thoroughly soaked take it out of the bowl and let the excess water drip off and then place it over the tray and press down so it touches the seeds firmly; it is a little larger than the shape of the tray, so pushing it down will cause the edge to fold up and form a paper rim around the tray, like a shallow rectangular dish made of papier-mâché.

If you can get it, use the ends of rolls of newsprint from your local newspaper for your covers. They're cheap, and you don't get your hands dirty with ink from the printed paper. Today's newspapers are printed with soy-based ink that doesn't contain lead, so it is safe to use regular recycled newspaper (printed newspapers are approved for organic gardening because the paper and inks are biodegradable and nontoxic). I just prefer the blank paper. It's a few dollars for about 2 or 3 inches (5.1 or 7.6 cm) of paper on the roll, and that will last quite a while. Of course with fewer newspapers actually getting printed every day, these rolls might get hard to find. The 24 inch (61 cm) size is just right cut into 12-inch

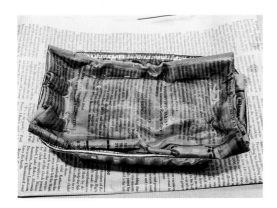

Cover the seeds with a soaked paper cover. Tuck the paper in around the edges so the paper is firmly touching the seeds. And don't be shy about pressing the paper into the edge of the tray.

(30.5 cm) strips right off the roll. Fold this as described above.

These covers can be reused several times and then recycled into the compost pile. When I first started to reuse the paper, I was worried that it might promote mold or other moisture-related problems, but after years of doing it I know it's OK. The covers become something of a solid block after the first soaking, but they still work well through several plantings.

If you keep your trays in a very dry spot, the paper cover may dry out before the 4 days are up. A room with forced-air heat, for instance, tends to dry the trays too fast. Be sure to check them on day two or three, and if the paper is dry pour a little water into the "container" it formed when you pressed it down into the tray. If drying out is a continuous problem, try using a thicker paper cover. The sprouts will still be able to push the cover up, and the extra paper will hold the moisture for longer.

Four Days of Darkness, and Other Incubation Techniques

With the tray planted and covered it's ready to spend the next 4 days in a warm, dark place. I love to tell people that the second step in indoor salad gardening is to "do nothing." You leave the soil sprouts alone for the first 4 days. I call it the incubation period—sort of like hatching an egg, the seeds need a warm, dark place to do their thing, which is to germinate.

The covered tray is now ready to stay in a warm, dark place for 4 days. My first choice is the cupboard over our refrigerator; it is warm and dark and handy at planting time.

You'll Need a Warm, Dark Place

It is important to find a spot that's at least 65 to 70°F (18–21°C) for this stage of growth. Let me restate that: If you want to harvest a batch of greens every 7 to 10 days, the germinating seeds need warmth to accelerate their growth. They'll grow in cooler temperatures, just not as quickly. Temperature is not as important once the seeds have germinated and grown an inch or so. When they're sitting on a windowsill greening up, the temperature can be 50 to 60°F (10–16°C) and they'll grow normally. If you look at seed germination charts, you will note a distinct temperature level at which the germination rate drops off quickly. In my workshops, when someone has sprouts that aren't growing as fast as mine, I recognize the symptom right away. I'll ask them how warm they keep their home and if they've found a cozy spot for germinating the seeds.

If you can provide only a cool place for the soil sprouts to grow, simply adjust your planting and growing cycles to maintain a routine, and you can still harvest fresh greens every day of the week. It is just that instead of 7 to 10 days, it will be more like 9 to 12 days until the shoots are ready to cut.

If you want to ensure the shorter growing times, be sure to provide a warm incubator of sorts for germinating the seeds. My number one suggestion is as simple as placing the trays in a cupboard over your refrigerator. It's both warm and dark and has proven a handy and reliable place for me. I also use a shelf in our windowless back hall located near the woodstove. A few more examples I've used or that friends have shown me include:

A cardboard box on a radiant-heated floor
A shelf near a space heater
Two drawers beside a dishwasher
An old armoire cupboard in a back hall
A closet near a chimney

With a little creativity you can find a way to give the seeds a warm, dark place. If you can't make it warm, then at least it should be dark. The paper cover will provide darkness for the first couple of days until the shoots begin to push up and loosen the cover, but I like to keep them in the dark all 4 days so the sprouts stretch and reach for the light. This is a key step.

During summer months the weather cooperates to provide warmth for sprouting, so the only issue is to provide a dark place, but take care to keep the trays away from cold drafts if you have air conditioning.

You Can't Mess This Up!

A few years ago I got a call from the chief food editor of a local newspaper. She was writing an article on growing greens in the winter and was reporting on her experience over the winter. A mutual friend had told her to talk with me. After I explained what I was doing she said that she wished she had found me 3 months ago because her article was going to press the next day with the conclusion that it is not possible to grow your own greens indoors over the winter months. She did print a blurb about what I was doing, but stayed with her original conclusion for a good reason: She had not found an easy way to grow all the salad greens you need throughout the winter months.

Fast forward to the fall of the same year, when I contacted her with an e-mail to let her know that I was presenting classes at the local food coop again and maybe she would want to give it another try, growing her fresh greens all winter. She wrote back that she was on her way to New Zealand for several months but asked if we could do an e-mail interview. One of her questions was, "Is it really as easy as you say?" It just so happened that the week before, my son Jake had dropped a tray of pea shoots, swept them into a dust pan, and promptly forgot about them. He had left the dust pan in a corner by our woodstove and didn't notice them for several days. We had taken pictures of this dust pan full of the pea shoots ready to harvest just a few days before she asked this question. It is almost impossible to mess this up. You can drop them on the floor, sweep them into a corner, leave them for days, and they still grow a crop. Unbelievable? Well just look at the photo!

In my classes you will hear me say "You can't mess this up," because there are many things you can do wrong and still manage to get a crop of fresh greens. The seeds want to grow, and given half a chance they will. By using soil to grow the greens it makes the whole process much more forgiving as well as more productive.

It has become a theme that I repeat often during a class. You can't mess this up! There are many things you can do wrong and still get a good crop.

After 4 days of warm darkness the sprouts are ready for light and greening the young shoots. In about 3 to 6 more days they're ready to harvest.

During a discussion on incubators in one of my classes, someone mentioned using a drawer beside the dishwasher, and I thought a nice dark drawer sounded like a great idea. I went home and put some of my own trays in a set of drawers up in my office. The following week the class was reviewing ideas for incubators when it dawned on me that I had forgotten all about the trays in the office. I went home and found three drawers full of shoots still yellow and more than ready for the windowsill. I watered the trays and put them on the sill, and they grew just fine.

This touches on a theme I repeat often in my classes—you cannot mess this up! The seeds want to grow, they are tolerant of mistakes, and anyone—green thumb or brown thumb—can grow an indoor salad garden.

Greening: Ready for the Light

After 4 days of growing in the dark, the young shoots should be about 1 inch (2.5 cm) high. They will have pushed the paper up, and their yellow heads will be peeking around the covers. I call it the "push-up day," and it is the sign that they are ready to come out of hiding and head for the sunlight.

When the soil sprouts have pushed the paper cover up about 1 inch (2.5 cm), they are ready to go into the light. Depending upon the temperature in the dark cupboard, this is usually about 4 days after planting. If the temperature is cool, around 55°F (13°C), then this may take an extra day or two to get the full growth, 1 inch (2.5 cm) high, we are looking for before exposing them to the light.

The soil sprouts are now ready for sunlight. They do not need southern exposure to grow and green up. The shelf in this picture is a small window on the north side of our house. You can tell that the sunflower and radish in this picture just came out of the cupboard because the seed leaf is still yellow. They will green up in a few hours.

And, yes they are more than strong enough to push the covers up while they're growing. You don't need to worry about smothering the plants with the heavy, wet paper covers. In the next few days, with regular water and a little light, the yellow leaves will turn green and the stems will grow longer. The indoor salad garden will become lush and ready to harvest.

Turning the trays every day will help the greens grow straighter, but since they'll only be growing in the light for a few days before harvest, that may not matter to you. They'll grow just fine even if they lean a bit.

When presenting to my classes I frequently hear "I don't have a southern window" and "I don't have good light," and these people assume that they can't grow shoots. This is another one of those cases where you have to unlearn what you know about gardening. The assumption is that bright southern light is an absolutely necessity. *It is not*. The light source for greening your soil sprouts can be any windowsill in the house. Direct sunlight is not a necessity; a northern window is just as good as a southern window.

It's even possible to green sprouts with the trays placed at a distance from the window, the same way that many a houseplant will do all right without direct light. Even light from a lightbulb, if it's lit for long enough periods during the day (about 6 hours), will work to green the shoots. (Note: I know this works with fluorescent and incandescent bulbs, but with all the new types of energy efficient lightbulbs, I can't say for sure. I have full-spectrum fluorescent lights in my office and no windows at all. My wife insisted on these special lights because she was convinced it was better for my health. It turns out that trays of greens like these lights, too, and they do just fine with no windows. I don't place them close to the lights by any means, but just on top of a three-drawer file cabinet.

So the light requirement for greening the shoots is very flexible. No excuses. You can do this!

You will find that different seeds have somewhat different preferences, though. Buckwheat likes direct sunlight best, which turns the stems pink or dark red. Pea shoots, in contrast, can do well in relatively low light. They'll even grow straight up in a dim, indirect light that would cause most shoots to lean toward the light source.

While electric lights can do the job, I want to emphasize that no electric lights are required, not ever. I relish the low-tech nature of this gardening method. It takes full advantage of our homes—places we keep warm, where there's light coming in through windows, and an ample supply of water piped in. I'll bet you never realized you were living in a greenhouse.

Windowsills

When I first started experimenting with indoor salad gardening, I greened on the sills of double hung windows in my kitchen and used the top mullion of the window sash (where the latch is) like a small shelf, too. The small trays fit on a relatively narrow windowsill, and the large trays fit most, but not all, sills. Of course, if you have casement windows or a large picture window, you'll have only the sill to work with.

As my garden grew I expanded to include the windows in the living room, then the family room. I could fit three small trays on a sill and two up on the window mullion on either side of the lock. My windows are 30 inches by 48 inches (76.2 × 121.9 cm) (an average-sized window), so I needed three windows to green fifteen trays of shoots in order to have fresh greens every day. This worked well for my family of four.

On any given day I have twenty trays in the cupboard over the refrigerator and fifteen trays greening on a window somewhere. This lets me cut five trays for salad daily, then I move five trays out of the cupboard onto a windowsill for greening, and lastly I plant five trays to go into the cupboard for 4 days of darkness, starting the process over again.

To keep track of which trays are which, there are a couple of strategies I use. Usually I just group the trays as I put them in the cupboard so each stage goes left to right; then after four days the four-day-old trays are ready to come out and be replaced by just-planted trays, each day moving to the right with the next batch. I have numbered my trays and color coded them. I have even tried using different trays for each day, like different cereal bowls. But the easiest way to keep track is to look at your greens. When the plants shoot up about an inch, they are ready to come out of the cupboard and go onto the windowsill. There are times when this stage will take an extra day or so, probably because of cool temperatures in the cupboard, so for this reason I recommend the eyeball test. Look and assess your "garden" to see which trays are ready. This is very much like what you would do in an outdoor garden: Look at your plants and see what they need and if they are ready for the next step.

I frequently get asked if it is necessary to keep the paper covers moistened day to day in the cupboard. The answer is no because the moisture of the paper is only essential while the seeds are germinating. Once the growing process starts—that is, the root goes down into the soil and the stem shoots up—the paper is of no use, so it can be dried out. The exception is if the paper dries out in the first 2 days because the house is exceptionally dry; then it would be good to rewet the papers. If this is a chronic problem, then use more paper for your covers and make sure they are sopping wet when you put them on the tray.

I bought this shelf from an unfinished furniture store to fit my window. With three coats of polyurethane on it to protect it from water, it has held up for many years. It mounted easily on the window frame with two screws.

Creating Shelves for Expansion

When I started experimenting I ran out of windowsill space. I was trying so many seed varieties; I would have as many as fifty trays at different stages needing to green on a windowsill. I needed more windows or more windowsills. I solved this problem in two ways: I bought some shelves first, and then I built some shelves. The store-bought shelves worked well, but there were only three shelves and my windows could fit four shelves. So when I built a shelf I made a few adjustments.

I built a shelf about 30 inches by 40 inches (76.2 × 101.6 cm) overall that fit over the front of a window, in effect adding more sills. After all the experimenting was done, it was a pleasant surprise that I was able to do all my gardening for my family with just one window and that one shelf.

If you like the idea, keep in mind that the height between shelves needs to be at least 10 inches (25.4 cm) so the greens have room to grow upward. You can hang a shelf with hooks and eyes, screw it into the casing boards, or even use Velcro strips rated for a few pounds of weight.

My own shelf sits on the windowsill and two screws attach it right to the wood trim around the window at the top. I built it out of 1 inch by 4-inch (2.5 × 10.4 cm) boards to fit the small trays. I built another one with 1 inch by 6-inch (2.5 × 15.2 cm) boards so I could include the larger trays that I occasionally use for pea shoots and sunflower greens.

In one of my classes a fellow told me he had decided to use large trays because they would take less time to plant. My question: "Will the large trays fit on your windowsills?" With an odd look that turned into a sheepish smile, he replied, "Oh, I didn't think of that." He was determined to use the larger trays, however, so he went home and built a shelf suspended in front of a window that would handle them.

This whole technique is so simple and easy to adjust, you can make it fit into your life the way you want it. You can start with using only windowsills for a small crop or expand by adding a shelf to a window and growing more greens.

How to Build a Shelf

Last year I was asked to present indoor salad gardening classes at a local Home Show in exchange for booth space. I wondered how to set up my booth so I could show exactly how little space it takes to grow 12 to 14 ounces (340.2–396.9 g) of greens every day. I wouldn't have a window at the booth, so I decided to build a shelf that would hold the trays for both the 4 days of incubation in the dark and the 4 to 6 days of growing in the light. What I came up with was a 20-inch-wide by 6-foot-high (50.8 × 182.9 cm) shelf. The cabinet at the bottom has three shelves about 6 inches (15.2 cm) apart, plenty of room for the first 4 days. There are four shelves for greening; I made them 6 inches (15.2 cm) wide to hold the large trays. This piece will hold about forty small trays at one time. There

I built this simple shelf large enough to both hold the trays for the 4 days of darkness and to green them for 3 to 5 days. There is enough room to plant and grow five trays a day every day year-round (or just for the winter months). This amount of space will yield 12 to 14 ounces (340.2–396.9 g) of fresh greens every day.

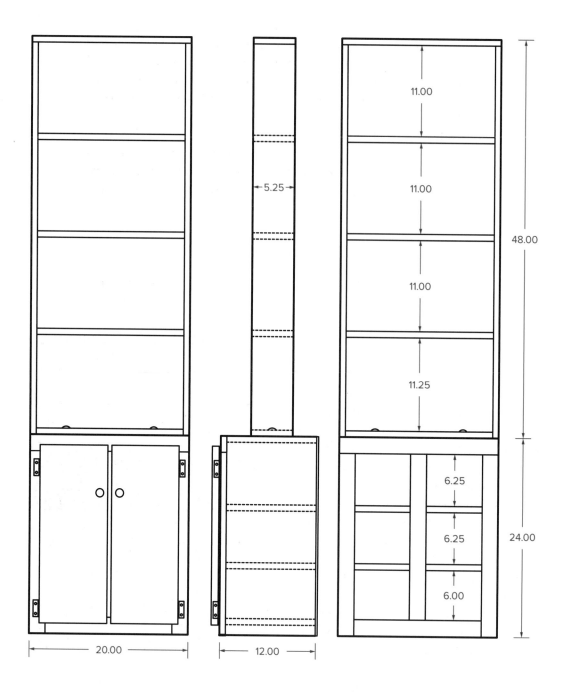

is space to plant five trays a day and extra space to leave five trays for an extra day if you don't harvest one day.

Building a stand-alone shelf might work best for your situation and is pretty easy to make. I built the one for the Home Show with just a cordless circular saw and drill. My son, who is a professional builder, shakes his head at my attempt to build a cabinet, but what can I say—it works. The building plans are a starting place and should be adjusted to fit your needs. For instance measure the window you plan to use and make the shelves the same width. Then measure the distance from the floor to the windowsill and make the base cabinet that height. Custom fit for your indoor garden.

The key points to building a custom shelf are making enough room to hold 4 days' worth of trays in the bottom cupboard and enough open shelf space to hold 3 to 5 days' worth of trays. If you have extra room for the trays with mature greens, you can add a few without a problem or you can skip a day.

Watering the Soil, Not the Greens

Once they're uncovered and placed in the light to green, each tray will need watering every day until harvest. For the small tray add 2 to 4 tablespoons (29.6–59.2 ml) of water a day. If you notice that the peat moss in a tray has turned light brown, the soil is too dry. If you tip the tray and water drips out, it's too wet! Extreme hot weather in the summer or a hot-air furnace or woodstove in the winter can affect how much water you'll need to add. Starting with well-moistened soil will make a difference, too. One way to judge if the tray needs water is to pick it up. A lightweight tray needs more water. If you check the weight of your trays before and after each watering, you'll begin to recognize when they're too light and too dry. It's a good way to double-check your schedule. After a week of watering and lifting, you'll be an expert at the heft test. The heft test works with either a ceramic tray or a light aluminum foil tray as long as you test it before and after watering to get used to the feel.

Water when you first put the trays into the sunlight, then water each tray with a few tablespoons of water every day after, just enough to keep the soil moist but not soggy. I like the watering can with a spout my son is using in this picture because the water pours right on the soil and not on the greens. I get questions in classes about misting the greens; I do not recommend this and prefer the water going directly to the soil and the roots.

If you brush the shoots with your hand, too, you'll get a feel for when the greens are becoming limp and need moisture. Then there is the finger test. Push your finger into the soil—if it feels moist, it's good; if your finger gets wet, there's too much water. If the soil is crispy and dry, you know you're overdue for water, and perhaps you should consider adding a little bit more water each day.

I'm often asked about drainage, and I insist it's not necessary. The trays I've been talking about have no drainage holes, and you don't need any if you're careful to water a little at a time. If you overwater, it's a simple matter to tip the tray and pour out the excess. Or you can even pull the whole mass of greens out of the tray and squeeze water from the soil like a sponge. I've already made every mistake in the book; you get the benefit of learning my tricks.

Water with small amounts every day, and you will eliminate the need for a pan under your trays to catch the excess (unless, as I noted in chapter 10, you're using peat pots that become saturated and tend to collect water underneath them).

If you do overwater the soil sprouts and the soil is soggy, just pull the whole planting out of the tray and squeeze the soil like a sponge! No really, I am not kidding, this works great and the plants don't mind a bit. Of course after you garden for awhile, you will get the hang of watering with just enough water and not too much.

You'll notice I have a system for every step of the process. My system for watering: A small plastic watering can with a long narrow spout is great for watering *the soil* and not the greens, which is what you want to do. Frequently folks ask about misting the greens, but that's not an effective way to get water into the soil, and it runs the risk of promoting mold on the sprouts. I recommend against it.

To make the whole process easier I place a watering can and a ½-gallon (1.9 L) jug full of water near each shelf of sprout trays, so watering daily is a quick and easy chore. As a matter of fact my sprout-watering routine mirrors the routine for my outdoor earth garden during the season. I do it when I get home from work. Instead of a chore it's a relaxing wind-down from a typical hectic day.

Hulls and "Brushing" Greens

Traditional sprouts, that is, those grown in jars, need to be cleaned of hulls before they're ready to eat. Soil sprouts tend to shed their hulls on their own, with only a little help needed here and there to get them ready for the salad.

Sunflower and buckwheat sprouts have big, hard hulls. Fortunately, after a few days of greening, they fall off on their own—most of them do, anyway. Not much turns off young salad eaters more than finding hulls in their food, so take the extra time to make sure you pick them *all* off when you harvest. While I'm watering the trays I'll often brush the greens with my open hand to loosen the hulls and encourage them to drop off. Every couple of days I sweep or vacuum up the hulls that have fallen around the shelf and on the floor.

If I'm in a hurry to harvest—if I want to gain a day and harvest sunflower sprouts ahead of schedule—I take the whole tray and run water over the greens to get the hulls off. I tip the tray sideways under the faucet to avoid soaking the soil, and with a trickle of water running over the greens, I pick at the hulls and they slip right off. Then I can put the tray back in the window where the sprouts will green up more quickly without their hulls. The extra effort is only necessary if you need that extra day. Of course you could plant a day or two earlier, but what would be the fun in that?

Looking at Soil Sprouts, Day by Day

There are key ingredients involved with getting a crop of fresh greens in just 7 to 10 days. In my classes I encourage folks to peek at their growing seeds, careful with the cover to lift up just a corner slowly so as to not

In just the time that the seeds are soaking, you can often see the first signs of the root forming within the seed. This is very prominent with the peas, but evident in most of the soaked seeds.

The roots orient quickly to gravity and head down into the soft soil. This is the beginning of that very important step of forcing the greens to reach for the light. As you can see, even though it has been just one day, there is considerable growth.

These radish seed roots blossom with root hairs ready to grab moisture to feed the plant. The root hairs on the radish are often mistaken for mold because of the dramatic white fuzzy appearance. Peas are not so dramatic; they seem to be in a hurry to send their tap root deep into the soil and have almost nothing for root hairs.

By the third day the stems have formed and are headed up in search for light. The seed leaves are still yellow without the light, but that is what we want at this stage. There is time for greening later; right now we want the stem to stretch. At this point the growth is uneven, but it will even out soon. The stems start to lift the paper cover.

uproot the tender seedlings. But it is so worth the careful peek to see how quickly they sprout and root. It is remarkable to see the development of the root hairs in just these first days. I have taken a series of photos to share this day-by-day sequence, a wonder to behold. One of the key ingredients of this technique is how the seeds are grown in the first 4 days. In the same way that a tulip bulb is forced to have flowers bloom for a specific holiday, we are forcing the seeds to become plants in just a week or so. By keeping them in the dark we start the soil sprouts

By the end of the fourth day, the stems are well formed, have pushed the paper up about an inch, and are ready to come out of the dark. Either at the end of day four or the beginning of day five, set the tray on a windowsill or shelf near a window. It does not need to be a south-facing window; if you can see there is enough light to green the soil sprouts.

As you can see in this photo, after only one day in the light, the yellow leaves turn green. Just one day. It is really something to behold; it still amazes me. When you put the tray on the shelf, you should water immediately.

The rapid growth continues to lengthen the stems and expand the seed leaves. A few tablespoons of water keep the soil moist and the greens growing.

At the end of day seven the greens are ready to harvest. They can continue to grow and fill out for another few days. This is when I think the tray resembles a head of greens, kind of like a head of lettuce, and is the start to a gourmet salad.

on a course to reach for the light, producing a long stem and full-sized seed leaf. This series of photos shows in detail this key ingredient.

If for some reason the sprouts have not pushed up like in the day-four photo, it is best to wait an extra day until they are about an inch high. The most common reason for slow growth is that the dark place they are growing in is not warm enough for rapid growth. Not to worry though—they will still grow, just not as fast. Warm means 65 to 75°F (18–24°C). That is why a spot like a cupboard over the fridge works so well, because the appliance is always generating some heat and warming the cupboard overhead.

When Are the Soil Sprouts Ready?

In my classes people ask me how long—after the initial 7 to 10 days—the sprouts can grow before the greens have to be cut. The answer is it depends. It depends which seeds, how rapidly the sprouts are growing, and what you will be using them for. If the radish greens look like the above picture, they will grow for another 3 days before you start to see some yellowing in the seed leaves. With sunflower greens you will notice the first true leaf begin to sprout between the seed leaves. At some point between when the hulls drop off and the true leaf appears is the best time to harvest sunflower greens. Buckwheat and broccoli are very slow to develop the first true leaf, so they can continue to grow for several more days with no loss in quality. Peas are at their most tender at 7 to 10 days, but if you intend to cook with them, they can grow up to 14 days in the tray. They may be 10 inches (25.4 cm) high by that time, but they will still be very delicious. The best rule is, as any good cook will admit, try some and see what you think.

CHAPTER 13

Harvest and Storage

Your greens are ready to harvest when the first small leaves—the seed leaf, or cotyledon—are fully grown and green and the stems are from 3 to 7 inches (7.6–17.8 cm) long. On average this stage arrives about 7 to 10 days after the seeds are planted. Refer to photos in chapter 15 to see what a fully grown seed leaf looks like. Another clue to watch for with the seeds that have hard shell hulls like sunflower and buckwheat is when the hulls have dropped and you see them on the shelf. Just remember that not necessarily *all* the hulls, just *most* of them, drop off when the soil sprouts are fully grown.

Also watch for the second set of leaves, the true leaves, to start forming. You will see them as a tiny set of new leaves growing where the two seed leaves join at the stem. Most true leaves are not as delicious as the seed leaf. In fact some are downright bitter, so cut your shoots as soon as you see the first sign of true leaves forming.

Pea shoots are an exception—they send up a stem with many true leaves right from the start, and they're ready to harvest when they're 6 to 12 inches (15.2–30.5 cm) high. Like a good cook you can taste them by nibbling a few shoots—it's the ultimate test for every variety.

Cutting to Harvest

When you're ready cut the greens about ¼ inch (0.6 cm) above the soil surface using scissors or a knife; I prefer scissors. When you're done cutting you should have a handful of greens with all of the stems lined up and ready to wash.

After 3 to 5 days of growing on the windowsill, the soil sprouts will be fully grown at about 8 to 10 inches (20.3–25.4 cm) high. Cut the greens about ¼ inch (0.6 cm) above the soil line. I keep the stems lined up as I harvest because I find it easier to wash and cut the greens, but if the greens get jumbled and tossed around, it doesn't really matter.

If the edge of your tray gets in the way of cutting, you can lift the whole thing—greens and soil cake—right out of the tray and set it on a piece of newspaper. This will give your scissors or knife blade better access to the bottom of the stems. I use this approach on all of my larger trays and on any tray where I can't easily reach the bottom of the stems.

If I manage to pull up stems with roots or dirt on them, it's easy to snip them while I'm still holding the freshly clipped mass and have the scissors right there in my hand. There's no problem with eating the roots as long as the soil is washed off, but I'm particular and like to snip off the roots.

Cleaning the Greens

Cleaning really starts before the greens are cut. Before grabbing the scissors inspect your sunflower and buckwheat and pull off any hulls still stuck to the seed leaves. Most of the hulls will have fallen into the dirt, but invariably some of them hang around among the stems or on the leaves. I am not greedy about my harvest and will pull the head right off a shoot if the hull doesn't come off easily. I've noticed frequently that sunflower shoots still encased in the seed hull by this time usually have a defect—a brown spot on the seed leaf. I don't hesitate to just pull those out and compost them with the used soil.

Once the greens are clipped first rinse their stems to clean off any soil transferred from the tray. Then soak the whole batch in a shallow pan of fresh water to clean them and remove any last hulls that are stuck on a leaf or hiding out in the greens. With larger seeds the job is quick and it's easy to get rid of big, unappetizing hulls.

For small seeds like broccoli or soft hulls like radish, it's a little harder to clean them off, but less critical, too. I use a simple technique: Place the shoots in a small shallow container (I use a 3-cup (710.4 ml) disposable plastic container that is 4 inches by 6 inches by 3 inches (10.2 × 15.2 × 7.6 cm) deep, but you can use whatever

Peas only need a quick rinse to get soil mix off the stems, but for radish, canola, and any soil sprouts that have hulls still stuck on the seed leaves, I use a small 3-cup (710.4 ml) flat plastic container. I push the cut greens down into the water, and the hulls float to the top. A quick tip of the container sends the hulls over the side. I repeat this action a couple of times to get the bulk of the hulls rinsed off, but a few small seed hulls are not any problem at all, so there is no need to go nuts trying to rinse every single tiny hull off. The sunflower and buckwheat are a whole different story because the hulls are large and unpleasant to bite into. I make sure these are all removed before I even cut the greens then rinse them.

you like in that size range); place the greens in the container and fill it with fresh water, letting the water run out slowly over the top; push the stems and leaves down to the bottom of the container, and the dry hulls will rise to the top and float off over the edge. Turn the whole batch of greens over, and repeat the process. This only takes a minute and works well for small seeds like canola or seeds with a soft hull like radish. It's not necessary to wash off each and every hull; they're soft enough to eat and have no flavor to speak of. But most of the hulls are left in the dirt, anyway.

Make a Salad, at Last

Let the fun begin! Picture this: You're standing in your kitchen surveying your garden asking yourself what will it be tonight—what looks ready to harvest? It's much the same as standing in the middle of your outdoor garden in July checking to see what's ready. You've accomplished in about a week of indoor salad gardening what would have taken a month or more outside. Not only do you have fresh greens, but they're beautiful— varieties of color, texture, and flavor ready for you to make a delicious salad or cook up a stir-fry for your rice or pasta.

Place the washed greens on a cutting board, and chop the stem end of the greens ¼ inch (0.6 cm) long. Toward the top leafy end of the stems, chop greens into larger 1-inch (2.5 cm) pieces if you want, but be sure to cut the stem into little bits. Sunflower greens are very tender and can be chopped a little longer, but I still cut them like the rest.

To get started place the washed greens on a cutting board and chop the stem ends ¼ inch to ½ inch (0.6–1.3 cm) long. Sometimes the stems of pea shoots and radish greens can have a very thin string, and cutting them into small pieces makes them crunchy with delicious flavor. The leafy tops can be chopped a little more coarsely—perhaps 1 inch (2.5 cm) long. They're all perfectly tender at this stage.

Toss all the chopped greens into the salad bowl. As you can see it is a beautiful salad; I call it the All-Star-All-Sprout Salad. This is the beginning of a future of fresh greens, homegrown for a fraction of the market price.

Mix the chopped greens in the salad bowl and serve. Our family usually has several dressings on the table to accommodate our individual preferences, and if there are leftover greens they'll store better in the refrigerator without dressing.

Once in a while, usually when we have company for dinner, my wife makes her special dressing and prepares it right in the salad bowl. It's pretty much a guarantee the bowl will be empty by the end of dinner. Make sure to check out chapter 16 for recipes. Enjoy!

Storage

When the greens are cut and cleaned but they're not going to be used immediately, put them in a plastic bag or container and place them in the refrigerator. They stay fresh and crisp for up to a week.

For a long storage life it's important to remove dirt, wash away the hulls, and let the greens dry off before bagging and chilling. There will still be some moisture on the greens. I don't literally dry them completely. A minimal amount of moisture in the bags helps them stay crisp in the refrigerator.

Store in the Tray

Before harvesting all the greens that are ready, consider leaving some where they are until you need them. Basically greens can be stored right in their trays. They continue to grow and require only a little water each day. They can stay in trays until their first true leaves (the tiny leaves that start to form between the big seed leaves) start to grow, at which point it's time to cut them no matter what. I'm not saying that cutting and storing them in the fridge is a bad thing, but there's no need for it if you use them fresh. No refrigeration means less space is required, which means you've decreased your carbon footprint. I live in a small cottage in the woods, and refrigerator space comes at a premium for me.

Green Bags

Recently I've been using Evert-Fresh Green Bags to store my sprouts. They're specially formulated to protect produce and retard spoilage (you can read about them here: www.evertfresh.com). Because I cut large quantities of greens ahead of time for my classes (every class ends with a salad), I like to do everything possible to keep the greens extra fresh. I use the bags for other garden produce, too, and even for bread with good results.

All Together Now

We've gone through each aspect of indoor salad gardening, and by now you've likely tried the Quick Start Guide on page 49 and you're planting trays of seeds. If you haven't planted anything yet, may I suggest that you begin with one or two trays and work up to as many as five trays a day? I admit this advice to start small is easier to give than to get. I've never been good at starting slow myself. If you're feeling like this might be a lot of work, go ahead, try growing just one tray a week to get the hang of it first—maybe one large tray, so you have a nice helping of salad greens.

Enjoying a small success is a good way to begin, and you'll be sailing along quickly enough, adding more to your garden every day. When I present classes I focus on one type of seed at a time, and everyone goes home with one planted tray for each session. It's easy to plant sunflower or radish once you learn how to plant peas, so one class is usually enough to get people started gardening.

In broad strokes a recap of the process goes like this:

- Soak your seeds and pour water into your soil mix to moisten.
- After at least 6 hours of soaking, the seeds are ready to plant.
- Fill your trays with compost, sea kelp, and moistened soil mix.
- Drain the seeds, and spread them over the surface of the soil so they just touch but do not overlap.
- Place a soaked paper cover over the seeds, and place the tray in a warm, dark place for at least 4 days (shoots will grow to about 1 inch [2.5 cm] high).
- Remove paper cover, water the roots, and place the tray on a windowsill.
- Water once a day until greens are ready to harvest, about 4 to 6 more days.
- Harvest by cutting with scissors or a knife.
- Serve in a salad, a sandwich, or a wrap, or use in a stir-fry.

The next step is to plant multiple trays, one for each variety of seed, creating a continuous supply of greens day after day. I regularly add two large trays of pea shoots in order to prepare a special recipe at least once a week. With my sons home I grow a few extra trays of sunflower greens, too. For my wife and me alone, I grow only two trays of salad mixes for a smaller daily harvest. You get the idea—start growing and adjust the amount to your needs. Whether it's for an army of hungry family members or just one person, an indoor salad garden easily fills the need.

CHAPTER 14
Soil Sprouts by the Numbers

O ne of my favorite workshop segments is the "numbers" discussion. I like to give folks a quick overview of sprouting by the numbers.

- If we plant 1 square foot (930.3 cm²) of shoots, we can expect to harvest 1½ to 2 pounds (680.4–907.2 g) of greens every 10 days.
- If 1 square foot is harvested every 10 days for a year, we will see thirty-six harvests and a total production of 54 to 72 pounds (24.5–32.6 kg) of greens annually.
- If we plant every day then it would be 547 to 730 pounds (247.8–330.7 kg) of greens harvested from a cupboard and a windowsill. We did not turn on a lightbulb, turn up a thermostat, have to pay more in taxes, or fire up a rototiller to produce this bounty of greens either.

Compared to other growing techniques—greenhouse, hothouse, hoop house, or hydroponics—indoor salad gardening is the most productive I've ever encountered. And it's a low-carbon-footprint, sustainable-agriculture model, as well. You can grow your own seed supply for the indoor salad garden, if you're so inclined, to sustain the growing cycle.

Yield Amounts per Tray

One small tray, 3 inches by 6 inches (7.6 × 15.2 cm), will yield about 3 ounces (85.1 g) of greens per planting. Of course the yield varies by the seed planted, but that's a good average for sunflower, radish, and pea. Expect about 2 ounces (56.7 g) per tray for buckwheat and broccoli.

On average I use about 12 to 14 ounces (340.2–396.9 g) of greens a day. The five trays I plant every day—one each of sunflower, radish, pea, buckwheat, and broccoli—typically yield 14 ounces (396.9 g) altogether.

So if you're wondering how much to plant, I suggest starting with five trays for a family of four. But if that seems like a lot, try one small tray each of sunflower and of peas per day. If you find you need more, add another tray of, say, radish, and keep adding varieties until you're satisfied with the daily yield. Start slow, learn as you go, and you'll feel more confident.

If you still need more, replace one of the small trays with a large tray, 4 inches by 8 inches (10.2 × 20.3 cm), of something like sunflower. This is what I love about gardening with these trays—it's an effective way to adjust the harvest according to your need, day by day and week by week.

Speaking of need take a look at your typical grocery list to determine your actual weekly consumption of greens. Your weekly purchase from the market should help you decide how many trays to plant at the start. For instance, if you are buying only a single head of lettuce a week, then you'll only use 1 to 2 pounds (453.6–907.2 g) of soil sprouts in a week for the same volume, or about two trays a day. Start with how much you want to harvest, and then do the math to figure out how many trays to plant.

Often in class people will say, "It's just for me." They either live alone or they're the only salad lover in the household. They know they'll only eat a serving of salad in a day (unless they're having salads for lunch). If it's just you, and you know that about 4 ounces (113.4 g) of greens a day will do, then consider planting one large tray of mixed greens daily. You can adjust the number and size of trays from that starting point as you get used to growing your own and you decide you want more or less. Have a little fun with mixes while you're at it. This can be a creative adventure, finding tasty and colorful varieties of seeds that suit you, since it is just for you.

Out of Pocket

My ballpark estimate for how much these greens typically cost me is under $2.00 per pound. That includes the cost of trays, soil, fertilizer, and paper. I calculate the soil and fertilizer and seeds as a repeat cost for each tray, using some new soil and fertilizer plus a new scoop of seeds each time I plant. I figure the trays are reused five times before I recycle them. So I calculate the cost of seeds, soil, fertilizer, and trays bought in bulk, with the cost spread out over months of planting. It is possible to reuse some of the soil for several plantings, and combined with the recycled trays (if you use ceramic bowls or other long-lasting trays, there is very little cost for trays), that helps to stretch the dollar. At the market today I can pay as much as $20.00 per pound for soil sprouts or fresh microgreens (I recently priced a 3-ounce [85.1 g] bag of greens for $4.29, which is just over $22.00 a pound) compared to about $2.00 to grow them. These savings are tremendous for a great low-calorie, nutritious food.

The Space Question

I sometimes forget to appreciate how tolerant my wife is of my gardening experiments. I have plants in trays all over our house. She has, and rightfully so, drawn the line a few times. But in general she gives me a long leash.

Folks in my classes sometimes say they could never have trays of greens "cluttering up the house." For you clutter-challenged folks, there is hope. You can create a stealth garden. Tucked among your houseplants and decorating your home, a complete indoor salad garden can grow, and no one will even know.

Start with beautiful ceramic pots that can hold one or two small trays, so you can just drop them in and place them among your decorative plants. The colors and textures of soil sprouts will contrast with aloe vera and spider, jade, or even cactus, and they look good right next to the amaryllis.

So when your housemates say, "Those plants look really yellow," you can let them know that they'll be green in just a few hours.

Or if someone queries, "What's this in the salad?" let them think it's something new you picked up at the store. They'll never know your secret. You'll be flying under the radar.

The Soil Sprout Season

Indoor salad garden season at my house runs from September, when the first frost is threatening to hit the outdoor garden, until the first greens start to mature in spring. That can be as late as May sometimes, if we've had a cold, wet spring. And sometimes during the summer my outdoor lettuces decide to bolt before my next crop is ready, so I plant a few trays indoors at the first signs of bolting and have a crop of shoots ready to fill the salad bowl.

For folks who don't have an earth garden outdoors, the indoor salad garden season is the entire year. You can fill the salad bowl spring, summer, fall, and winter with ease.

Reuse the Soil Mix

Often I get asked, when I am presenting a class, if the soil is reusable once the greens are cut. I reply with a question of my own: Do you want to do it to save money, to recycle, or to have a sustainable garden? If it is to save money, then consider that the cost of soil mix is under $0.10 for small trays. And treated as an expendable the soil could be recycled and not reused to be cost-effective; I hesitate to write "thrown in the trash" because in my home we fortunately don't accept that as a viable way to deal with things we are finished using. The idea is that to be economical about growing soil sprouts, you don't need to reuse the soil. Still, in an attempt to reuse, recycle, and garden in a sustainable fashion, why not try to reuse as much as possible! The answer is that it is easy to recycle the soil, and there are a number of ways to do it while indoor salad gardening.

There are several strategies to reuse the soil mix; the first and simplest is to recycle the soil and roots into a garden compost pile. I realize this option is not for everyone, but for those of us who have a garden outdoors and a compost bin, it is easy to incorporate the leftover soil with the daily compost run from the kitchen to the compost bin.

A compost bin needs a balance of greens and browns to decompose properly. Where I usually add straw or peat moss for the browns to balance out the greens from the kitchen scraps, the addition of the leftover roots and germination mix works well for the browns part of the formula. The formula, for those of you who are not familiar with compost making, strives to have one part browns to two parts greens. What does that mean? Browns refers to the nickname for carbonaceous materials that are usually dry and brown like straw or dry leaves. Greens depicts the fresh, moist nitrogen-rich stuff like green grass, green leaves, and kitchen waste. If you had a bucket of green stuff, then you would need half a bucket of brown stuff. Adding the soil cakes has a place in the compost bins, and even if your ratio of greens to brown is not perfect, it still should work well enough to make good compost. Especially in the winter the browns are hard to come by here in snow-covered Vermont, so the soil cakes are a welcome addition to the mix.

A compost bin can be filled completely with the soil cakes, and it will decompose perfectly without the greens from the kitchen waste (see the photo on page 46 in chapter 7). I used this second technique when I was growing a large quantity of greens and my regular bin could not keep up with the quantity of soil mix. The soil that I mix into my regular compost bin with the kitchen scraps I only use in the garden and not for growing soil

Use a 5-gallon (19 L) bucket with a lid to compost the soil cakes leftover from growing soil sprouts and shoots. Pack the bucket by pushing them down firmly into the bucket. Leave the bucket outside in the winter to expose it to the freeze/thaw cycles. Within a few months the soil will be broken down and ready to reuse.

Turn the masses of soil and roots, what I call soil cakes, over or onto their sides so they can dry out in the tray. Or put them on a drying rack if you have the room. But remember, as the soil dries, it will become crumbly and may make a mess underneath the rack.

sprouts. The reason is that compost made with kitchen scraps may promote mold on the soil, which will kill the greens within a day or two. This is too big a risk to use for growing greens. I have had good results from using the soil-mix-only compost; it is not loaded with the bacteria that promote molds that affect the tender greens.

In that same vein the third technique I have used is a 5-gallon (19 L) bucket with a lid stuffed full of only the soil cakes as a dedicated compost "bin." I left this outside exposed to the freeze/thaw cycles of winters here in Vermont. I was pleasantly surprised at how well this decomposed into a beautiful fine-soil mix completely usable for soil sprouts. It is hard to predict how long it will take to be usable again because there are so many variables. If you are growing five trays a day, it takes about a month to fill the bucket. As the bucket is filled push the soil down tightly, break the soil cakes up to fit pieces into each space between the square and round shapes of the cakes. Continue to add soil, pushing it down as hard and tight as you can, until the bucket is full. Seal the top with the lid. Once the bucket is full it will take a few months to cook—that is, break down the roots. Check the progress every once in a while, or just ignore the bucket entirely until you need more soil. There is no right or wrong way to do this. If you need the soil, go ahead and sift out the roots and reuse it for your next batch. Otherwise just let the bucket sit until the soil is a fine texture. You may have to sift out a few dried roots before you use it. If it is frozen, bring the bucket indoors for a few days to thaw.

After the soil cake is dry crumble it in your hand. As simple as that, it's ready to reuse. The soil will need to be moistened just like the original batch. If for some reason you have trouble with mold in a batch, it is best to use this soil for something else and start with a fresh batch of germination mix.

The fourth way to reuse the soil mix is to let it dry out completely. This might take a few days, depending on how wet the soil was when you harvested and how warm and dry the place is where they are stored. I turn the "soil cake" over in the tray so it airs out the bottom because the majority of the water is at the bottom of the tray and, thus, the soil cake. You will need extra space to store the drying trays of soil, of course, so it might not work if you live in tight quarters.

Some folks have also wondered if you can just replant right in the same tray as soon as the sprouts are cut. I have tried this, but it is not a good idea. Generally the decomposing roots and stems from the last batch promote mold and ruin the next batch. As tempting as it is I do not recommend this

It might be easier to sift the dried soil cakes instead of crumbling them in your hand. For a simple sifter using just a piece of hardware cloth, as shown in the photo, with a box or bucket will do the trick. This will separate the soil from the roots. It is then ready to reuse.

approach. But the other four strategies outlined above do work very well. So whether your intent is to save money or to recycle a resource, you will be covered using one of those four techniques.

Bringing Soil Sprouts into Schools

I have presented a number of classes just for kids, and there is no adequate way to express the wonder and enthusiasm kids bring to a simple thing like planting seeds, so I will instead tell a story. In one of my classes, presented in a lavish greenhouse, I sat on a wicker bench with a low coffee table in front of me. The kids gathered around it were seated on the floor. I demonstrated how to plant a tray.

Rather than spend time at the beginning explaining the how and why of planting soil sprouts, I like to start by planting a tray. And this technique is just as effective with older children as well; I just do it and let them see the thing done in a quick run through. Then I go back and plant another tray with more explanation.

In this class the parents stood behind the group or kneeled with their kids. The greenhouse air was heavy with moisture and the smell of earth, a perfect place for a garden class. One mom was kneeling with her daughter and raised her hand, like one of the kids herself; it was as if she were back in class asking permission to speak. She questioned me, "Why do you put the fertilizer at the bottom?" You may remember me discussing this in chapter 11.

It is a great question and one that I can rely on someone asking at this point in any presentation. As a gardener she knew that the fertilizer is usually mixed into the garden soil in an outdoor garden and wondered about putting it at the bottom of the tray instead of mixing it into the soil. I had a tray of mature pea shoots next to me on the low table, ready for this question. I pulled the plants out of the tray by the stems and turned them over to show the group the massive root ball that forms at the bottom of the tray. I answered, "This is why I put the fertilizer at the bottom; it is where the roots are."

The kid's wide-eyed reaction to pulling the whole bunch of greens out of the tray is fun to watch. It is such a surprising move and gets everyone's attention immediately. It brings the point home in a most graphic way. Maybe it is mischievous of me to do it, but it is such a great demonstration it is hard for me to resist! It is simple: Put the fertilizer where the roots are going to be in the tray.

This particular class had about thirty kids who ranged from 6 to 10 years old. One of the young girls in the front row noticed the roots forming on the soaked peas. I took the same tray of peas with the root ball, pulled them out of the tray again, and broke the soil cake in half so they could see the root that had come out of the pea and grown down into the soil mix.

Then I explained that the soil mix is important to hold moisture for the growing plant and that as we water the soil it provides moisture to the roots. I passed the open soil cake around for the kids to see. Kids seem to just love getting their hands in the dirt, and they relish having permission to explore. Every kid and many of the parents examined this revelation with keen interest.

At this point we put the seeds to bed with a wet blanket of soaked newspaper for a 4-day nap. I explained that wet newspaper replaces the top layer of soil that we usually cover seeds with in an outdoor garden. I showed them a tray of pea shoots with the cover sitting on top of them, the push-up day as I call it, to give everyone an idea of what the peas would look like in about 4 days. This also demonstrated what the shoots should look like before they go onto a windowsill.

The group broke up, and each kid planted his or her own tray of seeds to take home. At the end of this class I noticed five young girls comparing their trays and examining each cover. Apparently this was a birthday party activity for one of the kids. It was a precious sight to see.

As I thought back about this class, I realized it was in April, not in fall when indoor salad gardening generally starts. This class was intended as a primer for gardening in general and not so much for the kids to learn the specific techniques of my method. A number of teachers have told me that my technique is a great way to introduce gardening in general to children. In a very short time they plant, care for, and harvest a garden crop. It is a quick turnaround compared to planting in spring and harvesting in the fall. I have often heard about school garden project frustrations—that the kids lose interest, even the teachers lose interest in a garden plot at the schoolyard when the academic year ends. With indoor salad gardening the concepts can be introduced quickly and repeated as different curriculum agendas are addressed.

I am not a teacher, and I am not offering a curriculum by any means. But I can break down the points of interest that could be used to create one. As you pick apart the simple task of preparing, planting, growing, harvesting, and eventually eating the soil sprouts, there are a host of creative ways to use each step in the process to introduce basic concepts. There is an approach that educators have developed called "farming across the curriculum" that uses farming or gardening lessons to teach standard subjects. And there is no reason this approach cannot use growing soil sprouts as well. For instance, at the early elementary level, as the kids plant a tray, they will need to measure a tablespoon of seeds. That tablespoon can be used to learn volumes by measuring how many are in a cup and a gallon of seeds.

With the same tablespoon the weight can be measured and extrapolated to the cup and gallon. The kids can compare the relative weight of sunflower versus radish seeds. Then they will better understand why a 50-pound (22.7 kg) bag of sunflower seeds is much larger than a 50-pound bag of radish seeds! They can count how many seeds there are in a tablespoon of seeds and calculate how many would be in a cup, a gallon, even a 50-pound bag. The concepts of volumes, weights, and measures and using math skills as well can all be introduced just by planting a tablespoon of seeds.

When you add the soil to the tray, you can use the same measuring skills with the soil mix. The students can measure the perimeter of the tray and explore the concept of volume by calculating the cubic inches of the tray. Of course one of my favorite facts is measuring the square inches of a 3-inch by 6-inch (7.6 × 15.2 cm) small tray and then calculating how many trays make a square foot of trays and how many trays make an acre of trays. Maybe not for first graders, though! You probably know where I am going with this. The fact that an acre of trays can yield over 2 million pounds (960,000 kg) of fresh greens is a fact that continues to amaze me every time I tell my class this to let them know that it is a productive garden, albeit a small one.

As the kids plant they can make drawings of each step, and the older kids can make journal entries and sketch the process as well. They can use their journals or drawings to keep track of the days, record progress, and express their ideas and feelings about growing a garden.

The younger kids can weigh the greens while the older ones measure the results in servings of green leafy vegetables. They can calculate the servings needed for their class or even the whole school, then work backward to figure out how many trays they would need to feed themselves, the class, and their school community.

I get very excited about applying concepts to something tangible. I remember vividly the day I first used a 345 triangle to square a wall I was building; it was an aha moment. I had learned the concept of a right triangle in high school, but it had had no meaning to me other than another formula or factoid to memorize. When I used it to help me build the wall, it was thrilling. Connecting different areas of study to something as tangible as a garden and its harvest makes a lot of sense. We all eat—we all have an undeniable connection to a garden!

Certainly there is a wealth of opportunity for education in growing soil sprouts for the school curriculum. The seed itself has distinct parts. The ones younger kids can easily observe, with peas for example, will include the seed coat (testa); the thin green skin slips off the seed as it expands and grows. The root (radicle) appears early, sometimes even as the seed is soaked on the first day and buries itself into the soil. The seed leaf (cotyledon) splits open to allow the shoot (plumule) to grow upward. There are more parts to a seed, but these are the easy ones to observe while growing soil sprouts. And if you want to show the kids root hairs, plant radish seeds; they are distinctly spectacular—so white and fuzzy it is easy to mistake them for mold! As a matter of fact I try to remember to warn people about this in every class so they won't be shocked at the sight. It used to be the number one issue I would hear a few days after a class: "Help, my radishes are molding up at the bottom!" That is why I take pains to mention it now.

Growing soil sprouts can be used with older kids as well. Like a greenhouse, garden, and farm, the process can be used in similar ways to "soil sprout across the curriculum," and although it may not be as robust in its lessons as a farm process, it is still useful and can play a part. The soil sprout greens can be used the same as a greenhouse to supply a school kitchen with salads. By keeping careful records kids can compare the costs and income from their soil sprout garden versus the greenhouse, garden, or farm crops of greens. Comparing costs is certainly an important way to learn business and finance metrics. Certainly creating a business plan and connecting with the immediate community or collaborating with local businesses to supply greens are useful life lessons.

To explore sustainable alternatives the kids could look into the possibilities of growing their own seeds for crops like sunflowers and peas. They could research using different growing mediums; for instance they could make their own peat substitute by composting leaves from the community and using biochar to replace the vermiculite in the growing mix—very local and sustainable alternatives to growing any garden, indoors or out.

These are just ideas. As I said, I am not a teacher, nor am I qualified to create a lesson plan, but I am full of ideas that I hope will help teachers to create a plan of their own. As I researched gardening for this book, it was edifying to see how much interest in gardening has exploded over the last decade.

PART III

Seed Reference and Soil Sprout Recipes

CHAPTER 15
Seed by Seed

I tell the folks in my classes that they cannot mess this up. What I mean is, once the seeds are soaked they want to grow and will grow, given half a chance. I've made mistakes with my own seeds over the years, but despite anything I did the seeds still grew and provided a crop of greens. It's like a tiny drop of the driving force behind creation itself is captured in every seed.

Remember that what we are doing is a new, different way to eat seeds. Rather than boil, grind, or bake the seeds to make porridge, bread, or casserole, we are growing our seeds to prepare them for the table. Although this method is limited to certain seeds, there is still a wealth of variety to keep our daily salad interesting, lush, abundant, and delicious.

Five Basic Varieties

I use five basic varieties of seeds on a daily basis: sunflower, pea, radish, buckwheat, and broccoli. It's true that any one of these alone makes a good salad, but put them all together and they're a terrific salad.

Each seed has its own particularities and quirks, so it's worth giving them individual treatment in this reference. For instance I use several radish varieties and many varieties in the broccoli family for great greens. Others provide a little extra flavor or spice, like cress and arugula, which are too strong to eat alone. This reference will give you a working knowledge for how to plant, grow, and harvest each seed.

I also suggest some mixes of seeds that grow well together in the same tray for a distinctive blend of flavors. Mixes are a lot of fun. Consider designing your own to suit your taste and add some pizzazz to basic greens.

Some instructions here are simple—plant, grow, and harvest—for seeds like broccoli. Instructions for growing many varieties are similar, so I don't repeat all the details, but I have included a photograph of each seed type and mature plant, so you can see what you'll be working with and what you'll get in the greens.

Seeds like nasturtium and arugula grow very differently, however, and these varieties need careful explanation. Please note that I provide no Latin names in the seed reference. I don't use them and haven't found them helpful, so why pretend?

Do Your Own Thing

I continually try new seeds for my own soil sprouts. When you get comfortable with the growing techniques, you might want to try some of the other seeds mentioned and even a few entirely new seeds. When you do turn to something new, take the time to mark your tray with the name of the seed variety, the day they were planted, and the quantity of seeds you soaked. This information is helpful when making adjustments later on. You'd be surprised how easy it is to forget these little details even just a week later, especially if you try a couple of new things at the same time.

I encourage you to try growing whatever appeals to you with this method. Anytime I see a new seed in a catalog or online, I have to try it just to see what it's like. I list seeds here that I've tried, and I let you know my opinion of them to save you the trouble of growing awful-tasting greens.

Mung beans, winter and summer squash, zucchini, and pumpkin all have a bitter flavor as they develop into a leafy sprout, for example. Most available dry beans grow a bitter sprout, too, and they rot quickly. I haven't found any worth growing.

Millet is dry and grassy and has a bland flavor. While popcorn is very, very sweet, it also has a grassy texture and doesn't make for good eating, but it does grow a beautiful wide blade of grass with red stems, and I think it's worth growing just as a decorative green. Some people like to eat popcorn soil sprouts blanched, meaning the sprouts never go into the light for greening—they grow the entire time in the dark and are harvested and eaten still yellow.

Some shoots are delicious blanched (left in the dark) instead of greened, so be sure to try them that way as well. Have fun experimenting, and be sure to let me know what you discover!

Planting Setup for All Seeds:

SOAK ALL SEEDS:	6 to 24 hours; rinse before planting
INCUBATION TEMPERATURE:	70 to 80°F (21–27°C)
INCUBATION TIME:	3 to 5 days, wait until the shoots are ¾ inch to 1 inch (1.9–2.5 cm) tall
DAILY WATER:	2 to 4 tablespoons (29.6–59.2 ml) applied to the soil, not the leaves
GROWING TEMPERATURE:	50 to 70°F (10–21°C)

Seed Data

These are seeds that I find work beautifully for indoor salad gardens. Each one will provide a head of greens (that is, a tray full of lush greens that remind me of a head of lettuce) for your salad. We'll start with the basics: sunflower, buckwheat, pea, radish, broccoli, and a sixth tray for salad mixes.

Sunflower

SEED:	Black oil sunflower
AMOUNT:	1 tablespoon (14.8 ml) per small tray
IN THE DARK:	4 days or 1 inch (2.5 cm) high
GREEN:	3 to 6 days or until hulls fall off
YIELD:	3 to 4 ounces (85.1–113.4 g) per small tray
COOK:	Best fresh but can be used for wilted salad
HARVEST:	Cut with scissors ¼ inch (0.6 cm) above soil level
CLEAN:	Rinse with fresh water

Sunflower greens are a perfect salad ingredient, perfect for sandwiches, and great to nibble on all by themselves. If you grow one variety, it should be sunflower: crisp, tender, nutty flavor and just plain pretty.

DESCRIPTION

Sunflower greens are crisp and juicy with a delicious nutty flavor. They're productive, yielding 3 to 4 ounces (85.1–113.4 g) of greens from 1 tablespoon (14.8 ml) of seeds. Sunflower was the first soil sprout I tried, and it remains the base for most of my salads. I frequently grow an extra tray when my sons come home.

Nutritionally sunflower is rich in protein and vitamins A, D, B complex, and E. The sprouts are high in potassium, calcium, copper, iron, magnesium, phosphorus, and zinc, so like the raw seed, the greens are nutrient-packed.

SEED

Black oil sunflower seeds are the best for shoots. If you can see the seeds before you buy them, look for a nice almond shape about ¼ inch (0.6 cm) wide. Check for cracked or hulled seeds in the batch. A few are tolerable, but these will almost certainly not grow, and more importantly they may cause rotting or mold in your tray.

If you see striped seeds, they're the wrong variety. I've received seeds that were particularly small from a reputable seed company. I was disappointed because the seed leaf, of course, was small, too. The flavor was good, but production was down. So try a little before you buy the big bag.

Although the giant striped sunflower (sometimes referred to as confection sunflower) grows pretty well, the shoots hang on to their hulls so you have to pluck nearly every one. Even more importantly to my mind they don't have the rich, nutty flavor of black oil seeds, but if they're all you can get they still make good greens for the salad bowl.

SOW

When I first started growing sunflower I took the trouble to plant each individual seed with the pointed end down in the soil. This is what I would do outdoors, and it made sense to me. I have long since stopped that and now just scatter the soaked seeds over the top of the soil so they touch but don't overlap each other.

GROW

Keep in the dark 4 days before placing in the light. Wait an extra day if the shoots are not up a full inch (2.5 cm) before putting them in the light. Turn the tray daily when you water so they don't lean toward the light source and fall over. Harvest after the seed leaves spread out and drop the seed hull, about 4 days after setting out into the light. When the first true leaves start to show, it's time—you must harvest. They will become bitter and fuzzy if left to grow too long. From the first sign of the true leaves in the notch between the big seed leaves, you have at most 3 or 4 days before these fuzzy, bitter stems and leaves grow.

HARVEST

Just before harvesting is a good time to pick off any hulls. Pull out short shoots that contain hulls tightly wrapped around the leaf, too. These will almost certainly have brown leaves inside. (I don't think they're worth the trouble to try to save them. Try plucking the hulls off and see if you agree with me.)

With scissors cut the stems ¼ inch (0.6 cm) above the soil. I pull the greens and the soil cake right out of the tray so it's easy to access the stems.

CLEANING

Sunflower sprouts are easy to clean; just a quick rinse in clean water is all it takes. If you submerse the greens in a bowl of fresh water, any remaining loose hulls will float to the top. Try to get them all off. No one likes to crunch on a dry sunflower hull in a salad.

COOK OR FRESH?

Sunflower greens are best fresh for salad but can be used in a wilted salad; they are too tender for a stir-fry.

TROUBLESHOOTING

Sunflowers don't like their feet wet, so be careful not to overwater. If the soil does become saturated, pull the cake out of the tray and squeeze it like a sponge. If you notice that your sprouts look and feel limp even though the soil is moist, the soil is waterlogged.

SPECIAL TECHNIQUE

I was once in a big hurry for a harvest of sunflower greens. My stepdaughter asked me to grow greens for a dish she wanted to make for her daughter's graduation. I had 6 days total—it was Friday evening when she asked me to grow them, and she needed them the following Friday.

I soaked the seeds overnight—about 14 hours—until I saw shoots starting to poke out of the hulls. That was Saturday morning around 11:00 a.m.

I planted the seeds as usual but placed them in an extra-warm cupboard. It was June, so that was easy to do, but in winter I might have gone to the extra effort of using a grow mat or finding a spot near the furnace or the woodstove. A dark spot that's kept at 70 to 80° F (21–27° C) is called for.

I let the sprouts grow in the dark until they were 3 or 4 inches (7.6 or 10.2 cm) tall. That needed 6 full days, which took me to Thursday evening before I removed my greens from the cupboard. In order for the leaves to green quickly, all the hulls had to be removed. With all of the hulls removed from my greens, I put them under a fluorescent light that was set about 3 inches (7.6 cm) away from the tops of the sprouts. I use that light to grow garden sets, but even an incandescent bulb would have worked. I left the light on all night, and by Friday morning the trays were ready to harvest. Presto!

This was an extreme circumstance, but it worked in a pinch.

GROW YOUR OWN SEEDS

Growing sunflowers for seeds is easy. I figure that a 200-foot (61 m) row of flowers yields enough seed to last me a whole year—about 5 to 6 gallons (19–22.8 L) of seeds.

The biggest problem will be the critters that love to eat the seeds. Birds, squirrels, and chipmunks all love sunflower seeds. The simplest way to protect the seed head is to cover the flower with a paper bag. The seeds will still ripen even with a bag on the flower head. Sunflower is an annual, so you can expect a harvest the same year you plant.

When the seeds are fully formed cut the stem of the plant below the flower head and dry it in a shaded, covered spot protected from rain and critters. Once dry the seeds can be stored right in the flower head but are more likely to retain viability if you remove them, dry them, and store them in a glass jar.

Buckwheat Lettuce

SEED:	Common buckwheat, unhulled
AMOUNT:	1 tablespoon (14.8 ml) per small tray
IN THE DARK:	4 days or 1 inch (2.5 cm) high
GREEN:	4 to 7 days or until hulls fall off
YIELD:	2 to 3 ounces (56.7–85.1 g) per small tray
COOK:	Only fresh or wilted, cannot be cooked
HARVEST:	Cut with scissors ¼ inch (0.6 cm) above soil level
CLEAN:	Rinse with fresh water; check for hulls

DESCRIPTION

Lettucelike, delicate, tender stems with a distinct sweet-and-sour flavor, the pale pink stems and green leaves of buckwheat make this a versatile green that is just as good in a sandwich as it is in the salad bowl. If the sky is cloudy for the first few days the tray is on the windowsill, stems will be white, but with plenty of bright sun during those days, you see pink to bright red stems. They taste the same, though, whether white or pink. Buckwheat doesn't mind if the soil dries out a bit, but it will stop growing if the soil gets soggy. The greens contain the bioflavonoid rutin that is not found in beans or other grains and the amino acid lysine that is not found in most other grains.

Seed

Common buckwheat is a mixture of the two distinct varieties, Mancan and Manor, and as the name implies, it's the most commonly available. For our purposes there's no difference in the named varieties, and any source of organic seed is suitable. Be extra careful. These seeds are sensitive to heat and moisture and will lose viability quickly if not stored in the dark in an airtight container like a Mason jar. Consider keeping your bulk seeds in the refrigerator or even a freezer, and keep, at most, only a quart jar out for planting. Or buy small amounts of fresh seeds at a time.

Buckwheat has lettucelike, delicate, tender stems with a distinct sweet-and-sour flavor. The pale pink stems and green leaves of buckwheat make this a versatile green that is just as good in a sandwich as it is in the salad bowl. If the sky is cloudy for the first few days the tray is on the windowsill, stems will be white, but with plenty of bright sun during those days, you see pink to bright red stems.

SOW

When you spread buckwheat out over the soil, make sure the seeds don't mound up but are spread evenly. By their shape and size you should be able to lay a tablespoon (14.8 ml) of them per tray so that the seeds just touch. I use an extra paper cover or an extra-thick cover for buckwheat. They seem to sprout more consistently if the cover remains moist. If it dries out early in the incubation period, seeds around the edges sprout more slowly than those on the interior and the tray of greens grows unevenly, with different sections at different stages of development.

GROW

Bright light the first day out of the dark incubation period produces a red stem that looks nice in a salad but doesn't change the flavor. Wait until the whole tray of seedlings is 1 inch (2.5 cm) high to take the tray out of the dark and put it in the light. By giving the tray this extra time, the growth is more even in the tray and the hulls drop off in concert as if on cue from the conductor. Let the sprouts grow until most of the hulls have dropped off the seed leaf.

HARVEST

First pick off any hulls still attached and pull out the short shoots that still have a hull tightly wrapped around the leaf. To remove hulls from ready-to-harvest sprouts, squeeze the triangular-shaped hull and it will break and come off the leaf easily with a slight twist. With scissors cut the stems ¼ inch (0.6 cm) above the soil.

This picture illustrates the variation that the buckwheat stems can have depending on the amount of sunlight they get in the first few days on the windowsill. Bright sunlight makes the stems pink to dark red, and cloudy days leave the stems white. Both have the same delicious flavor.

CLEANING

Buckwheat needs only a quick rinse in clean water. Double-check that all of the hulls are off the leaves—they can be sharp. To be certain all of the hulls are gone, soak the greens in a bowl of water, push the whole batch under the water, and let the hulls rise to the top where they are easy to pour off.

COOK OR FRESH?

Buckwheat lettuce is for fresh use or in a wilted salad. These shoots are so tender they're perfect to load up in a sandwich or wrap.

TROUBLESHOOTING

The good news is that buckwheat sprouts will drop nearly all of their hulls on their own, so the sprouts are easy to clean. The bad news is that they drop their hulls on the shelf and floor. (I keep a Dust Buster nearby to pick up around the trays and keep everything tidy.)

If you get uneven growth within the tray, try adding an extra layer of newspaper to hold moisture in during the incubation period and give them an extra day of dark incubation. Watch out in very cold weather that the leaves do not touch a very cool windowpane.

SPECIAL TECHNIQUES

Buckwheat benefits from warm incubation temperatures, but the greens are very tolerant of a cool room for growing. They are very tolerant of dry soil but wilt if you get the soil waterlogged.

GROW SEEDS

Buckwheat is relatively easy to grow outdoors for seed. Plant in July when the soil is warm, and it'll flower and bear seeds in the cooler nights of September. Buckwheat is not frost hardy, so plan to harvest before the first drop in autumn temperatures. A 200-foot (61 m) row about 1 to 2 feet (30.5–61 cm) wide broadcast with seeds will yield about 30 pounds (13.6 kg) of new seed. That should easily last a year of daily plantings.

Pea Shoots

SEED:	Snow pea
AMOUNT:	1 tablespoon (14.8 ml) per small tray
IN THE DARK:	3 to 4 days or 1 inch (2.5 cm) high
GREEN:	4 to 10 days or until hulls fall off
YIELD:	3 to 4 ounces (85.1–113.4 g) per small tray
COOK:	Excellent fresh or cooked
HARVEST:	Cut with scissors ¼ inch (0.6 cm) above soil level
CLEAN:	Rinse with fresh water, no hulls

DESCRIPTION

Pea shoots are the workhorse of soil sprouts. They're easy, productive, and tolerant of cool temperatures. They're crispy and sweet and just as good in a fresh salad as they are cooked in a stir-fry. Pea shoots have a long history in Chinese cuisine dating back some 5,000 years. This is a versatile seed that's great for kids to start with because it's easy to grow and dramatic changes are visible day to day.

Pea shoots are the workhorse of soil sprouts. They're easy, productive, and tolerant of cool temperatures. They're crispy and sweet and just as good in a fresh salad as they are cooked in a stir-fry. Pea shoots have a long history in Chinese cuisine dating back some 5,000 years. This is a versatile seed that's great for kids to start with because it's easy to grow and dramatic changes are visible day to day.

Seed

The variety that I grow is a snow pea; it's the one used in Chinese cooking, flat with no full, round peas in the pod. A friend in China said it's what they grow there, and I've had good success with the variety. It grows tall with a tender stem and lots of green leaves. Almost any variety will work, though; I've tried them all. I don't particularly like the dwarf varieties often listed in seed catalogs for shoots, but they work just fine, too. I just happen to think the snow pea is more vigorous and productive.

Sow

Scatter 1 tablespoon (14.8 ml) of soaked pea seeds on top of the soil. It's best to weed out the broken and off-color seeds now—they won't grow and will rot on top of the soil. Peas will soak up a lot of water in the first 6 hours, so make sure the dry seeds are covered with an extra measure of water at the very beginning to keep up with the swelling peas.

GROW

Pea shoots can tolerate low light as well as cool conditions and still produce a good crop of greens. I've grown them in the middle of my kitchen with no extra light. When you water peas pour the water on the soil and not over the stems and leaves. You do not need to turn the tray of peas, they seem to grow straight up even when lighted from a bright window.

HARVEST

If you're planning to cook the greens, you can let them grow very long, as much as 14 inches (35.6 cm) high, but for fresh salads cut them at 10 inches (25.4 cm) at about ¼ inch (0.6 cm) above the soil line.

CLEANING

Pea shoots barely need anything more than a quick rinse under the faucet. There are no hulls to pick off or wash off, so these greens are remarkably easy to clean.

COOK OR FRESH?

Add chopped pea shoots to a fresh salad. Use them as wilted greens, adding them to stir-fried vegetables just before removing them from the heat. Or serve pea shoots over rice as the featured vegetable, sautéed with onions, garlic, and mushrooms.

TROUBLESHOOTING

Pea shoots are virtually trouble free. They grow tall, so at some point they may fall over, but it makes no difference in the quality of the greens. They naturally grow very straight, so even if you don't rotate the tray, they still stand upright. Remember that the longer the shoots grow, the tougher and more stringy the stem will be. You can cut these stems in ¼ inch (0.6 cm) pieces to minimize the toughness in a salad or stir-fry. If you plan to cook and serve them whole, cut them when they're only 6 inches (15.2 cm) high and the stems will still be crisp and tender. It is a special treat, though, because the tray won't be as productive when you clip early.

SPECIAL TECHNIQUES

Most soil sprouts are a one-shot deal—sow, harvest, compost the soil, and replant. Peas are the exception; they will grow another shoot after the first is cut. Don't look for large harvests from the second crop, though. In my first series of classes one of my neighbors brought his tray of pea shoots back with him each week to demonstrate how they continued to grow right through the 5 weeks of class. By the fifth week he was getting pea shoots the size of match sticks, but that didn't seem to matter to him; he was delighted with the harvest.

GROW SEED

Peas are an easy-to-grow annual that produce bountiful crops of pods. The pods should be left on the vine until the stems start to turn brown. Harvest by cutting the whole vine and hanging it in a shaded location protected from rain. A garage or toolshed is perfect. When the seeds are hard and wrinkled, they are ready to store. A 50-foot (15.2 m) row of trellised peas should produce about 30 pounds (13.6 kg), enough to last a year.

Radish Greens

SEED:	Daikon radish
AMOUNT:	1 tablespoon (14.8 ml) per small tray
IN THE DARK:	3 days or 1 inch (2.5 cm) high
GREEN:	3 to 6 days or until hulls fall off
YIELD:	3 to 4 ounces (85.1–113.4 g) per small tray
COOK:	Best fresh or wilted
HARVEST:	Cut with scissors ½ inch (1.3 cm) above soil level
CLEAN:	Rinse with fresh water

DESCRIPTION

Radish greens are spicy hot when sampled from the tray, but they lose most of their heat when mixed with a salad dressing and other greens. They are the fastest-growing seeds and make a beautiful, full, lush head of greens.

People who don't like the vegetable radish probably won't like radish greens, either. The impression I get from students in my classes is that many people like the hot stuff! It's amazing how much flavor one single shoot of radish can have. Try it—just clip off one stem and see what a burst of flavor you get. Radish is loaded with vitamin C, like citrus fruit. Captain James Cook in the 1700s used sprouts as well as limes to prevent scurvy, a vitamin C deficiency, on long sea voyages.

SEED

There are several radish varieties that are great, vigorous plants. Daikon radish has white stems and big seed leaves. China Rose has multicolored stems—red, pink, and white—but isn't as large as the daikon. Hong Vit is a lot of fun to grow and use in a salad, with its bright red stem and deep green leaf. There's even a purple radish, which is OK but looks black in a

Taste just one tiny stem of daikon radish and you will be amazed at the full radish flavor *and* heat. Once mixed into a salad with dressing, the heat is tamed and the radish flavor comes through. There are many varieties worth growing, but daikon is hardy and inexpensive. Radish sprouts grow fast and can be harvested in as little as 6 days.

salad, so I don't grow it very often. It's a tough choice with radish—so many varieties are excellent for growing shoots. My vote goes to the daikon radish. It's always hearty and green with fat juicy white stems and large leaves—and it is reasonably priced.

Sow

Anywhere from a tablespoon (14.8 ml) to a heaping tablespoon (22.2 ml) works for a small tray. The heaping tablespoon will produce more but the larger quantity sucks up water really fast. I use a regular table-spoonful and plant often for a steady supply. Spread the soaked seeds over the soil so

Like its daikon cousin, Hong Vit is easy to grow. The seeds are much more expensive, but the brilliant pink stems and deep green leaves make the soil sprouts eye candy in the dead of winter. Oh so worth it!

they touch, and if you are using the heaping tablespoon of seeds, they will even overlap some. Try for an even layer of seeds on the soil.

GROW

Radish sprouts grow rapidly and sometimes are ready to go into the sunlight in just 3 days. When watering radish I recommend that you water the soil—that is, pour the water into the tray along the side so the water flows across the soil and sinks in, rather than sprinkling water over the tops of the greens. If too much water sits on the leaves of radish greens, they develop black spots that ruin the crop. Although this is the watering technique I recommend for all the soil sprouts, it is especially important with radish.

HARVEST

Cut the stems about ½ inch (1.3 cm) above the soil line to avoid the seed hulls that have dropped on the soil. Check for clumps of radish seeds that stick to the stems and pick them out. Don't bother to pick the hulls—they're easy to wash off.

CLEANING

Clean in a smallish shallow tray, about 6 inches long and 2 inches deep (15.2 × 5.1 cm), filled with fresh water. Push the greens down, and the hulls will float to the top. Pouring off a little water will take the hulls over the edge. Continue this action a few times until most of the hulls are gone. The hulls don't have a strong flavor so it's OK to leave a few.

Broccoli, the Cole Family, and Asian Cousins

SEED:	Canola is my first choice
AMOUNT:	1 teaspoon (4.9 ml) per small tray
IN THE DARK:	5 days or 1 inch (2.5 cm) high
GREEN:	4 to 6 days
YIELD:	2 ounces (56.7 g) per small tray
COOK:	Fresh, cook in tempura, or add to soup
HARVEST:	Cut with scissors ¼ inch (0.6 cm) above soil level
CLEAN:	Rinse with fresh water in a shallow tray

DESCRIPTION

I started working with broccoli after my first year of growing soil sprouts. I had read several articles on the health benefits of vegetable broccoli, and every time an article said how good it was, it also mentioned something like "broccoli and broccoli sprouts," so I was intrigued to see if I could grow the sprouted version with my soil sprout technique. I had to make only two small adjustments. First I used only a teaspoon (4.9 ml) of seeds instead of the tablespoon (14.8 ml) I usually use for a small tray. Second I extended their time in the dark by a day. And they grew perfectly.

I went nuts and bought every broccoli-family seed I could find, including the Asian family of coles like bok choi and mizuna. They all plant exactly the same way, using just a teaspoonful for a small tray, with the extra day—that is, 5 days—in the dark before greening on the windowsill. Now I usually plant one tray from the broccoli family in my daily schedule.

Purple kohlrabi is one of my cole family favorites with its bright violet to lavender stems and deep green leaves, so beautiful in a salad. Just when the world seems dull in the winter, here's a brilliant color growing on the windowsill and gracing the salad bowl. If you have trouble with the seeds bunching up in the middle and growing up in clumps, just run your finger down the middle of the tray after spreading the soaked seeds on the

The photo shows 4 pounds (1.8 kg) of vegetable broccoli to illustrate how potent the tiny broccoli soil sprouts can be. One ounce (28.4 g) of broccoli soil sprouts can have as much of the cancer-fighting antioxidant sulforaphane as the 4 pounds of vegetable pictured. An ounce of prevention.

The bright violet to lavender stems and dark green leaves make purple kohlrabi a stunning addition to a winter salad. Like organic broccoli, it is an expensive seed by the pound, but just a teaspoon makes a whole tray of greens. I add it to my Red Mix for a showy gourmet salad.

Canola is a vigorous growing soil sprout and my first choice for an everyday addition to the salad from the cole family. The seeds cost a lot less than organic broccoli seeds, too. Canola has the same subtle sweet flavor and can be used in cooked food the same as all the cole family.

soil. This ¼-inch (0.6 cm) gap in the middle of the tray solves that problem. The tiny greens do not need as much water as the larger seeds like sunflower, so adjust the watering when you come to the cole family tray.

Sometimes called poor man's cabbage (but I call it poor man's broccoli), canola is rewarding to grow, maturing quickly, with a brilliant white stem and a distinct yummy flavor. As the nicknames would indicate, the seeds are the least expensive of the cole family.

Broccoli is not as productive as the other four seeds in my basic indoor garden, yielding barely 2 ounces (56.7 g) per tray as a typical harvest. Still it seems very worth growing to me for the colors, texture, and nutritional value it adds to the meal. When I make soup I like to clip a pile of broccoli greens to drop on top for a garnish just before serving. Not only are they delicate and pretty, but they also provide a powerful nutritional boost even in small quantities. The book *SuperFoods Rx*, by Steven G. Pratt, M.D., and Kathy Matthews (HarperCollins, 2004), includes broccoli sprouts because of the enormous quantity they provide of the antioxidant sulforaphane, which actually attacks cancer in the body.

SEED

The first thing you will notice about cole-family seeds is how tiny they are! They are perfect, little dark purple or black balls barely even ¹⁄₁₆ of an inch (1.6 mm). For my everyday plantings I use broccoli, canola, and purple kohlrabi. Canola is an inexpensive broccoli cousin. It's called "rapeseed" in Europe, but according to Sheri Coleman, director of marketing for the Northern Canola Growers Association, canola is a variant developed in Canada to extract the oil, and it's genetically different from rapeseed. Despite the fact that the plants are the same species, rapeseed is bitter and considered inedible as a seed and as a soil sprout.

And purple kohlrabi is the beauty queen. I discuss all of the cousins at the end of this section. They're all planted, greened, and harvested the same way.

Sow

The big difference with these tiny seeds is that you only need 1 teaspoon (4.9 ml) for a small tray. As a general rule you can plant about one-third of the amount you'd plant in large seeds for all of the broccoli family—one teaspoon, rather than a tablespoon. (It is a good thing, too, since most of the broccoli family is expensive.) I dump the seeds out onto the soil in a tray and then use the back of a spoon to spread them around evenly. A spoon works better than fingers. The small, wet seeds don't stick to the metal the way they do to skin.

Grow

Most of the broccoli-family greens take an extra day or two of dark to grow the first inch. It's worth the wait. Once they're in the light they shoot up quicker if they've had this extra time in the dark. The growing cycle is a bit longer with most small seeds, actually. What is a 7- to 10-day cycle for the larger seeds is 10 to 14 days for the little ones.

Harvest

I pull the soil and greens right out of the tray to cut broccoli greens. Just tug the soil cake out whole. This technique makes it easier to clip their stems close to the soil line.

Cleaning

Place clipped greens in a small tray about 1½ to 2 inches (3.8–5.1 cm) deep. Fill the tray with water, and push the greens down to the bottom. The little black balls that are the hulls will pop to the top and spill over the side when you tip the tray. Or keep the water running into the tray at a drizzle so you can submerge the greens and spill the hulls continuously. Turn the whole mass of greens over to get at any hulls that are trapped underneath; repeat. After this they should be ready for a salad.

Cook or Fresh?

All of the broccoli-family greens are terrific in a salad. And they hold up well when deep-fried in batter. I use them clipped and sprinkled on top of a hot soup as a nutritious garnish.

TROUBLESHOOTING

When sowing try not to leave the seeds in clumps. They'll get pushed right off the soil and end up stuck together on the stems of surrounding greens. They won't grow, and all you can do when you're harvesting is cut them out. Take a little extra time to spread the seeds thinly and evenly on the soil to avoid the problem in the first place; using the back of a spoon helps to spread the seeds evenly.

SPECIAL TECHNIQUES

If you have recurring trouble with molds in the middle of your trays in warmer weather, try running your finger or the edge of a spoon down the middle of the tray when you plant the seeds, creating a furrow so no seeds grow down the center. This little trick has worked great for me. It allows a little more air circulation among the greens when I put them in the light, and that seems to be just enough to prevent mold.

GROW SEEDS

Most broccoli-family plants need 2 years to produce seeds, so it's out of the question where I live in the north to grow them for seed. But if you grow them in warmer climates, keep in mind: As with other plants providing seeds for sprouting, you don't have to worry much about cross-pollination. They will only be used for sprouts, so you don't have to isolate the plants as you would if you were growing seeds true to type. Since I haven't grown broccoli for seeds, I can't give you an estimate for how much to plant.

If you venture in, let me know how it goes.

Seed Mixes

SEED:	Mixture of varieties of seeds like sunflower and buckwheat
AMOUNT:	1 tablespoon (14.8 ml) per small tray
IN THE DARK:	4 days or 1 inch (2.5 cm) high
GREEN:	3 to 6 days
YIELD:	2 to 3 ounces (56.7–85.1 g) per small tray
COOK:	Best fresh but can be used for wilted salad
HARVEST:	Cut with scissors ¼ inch (0.6 cm) above soil level
CLEAN:	Remove large hulls; rinse with fresh water in a shallow tray

DESCRIPTION

I started experimenting with seed mixes for two reasons. The first was my wife, who asked me to figure out a way for her to bring a salad to work

More on the Broccoli-Family Greens

Canola

Canola is my first choice from the broccoli family. Easy to grow, the greens have a strong cabbagelike flavor, and the bright white stems quickly grow long and straight. They're a crisp addition to the salad. I call canola the poor man's broccoli because the seed is about half the price of broccoli seeds.

Purple Kohlrabi

Purple kohlrabi is a favorite for its bright purple stems and dark green leaves. When you chop these into a salad in the dead of winter, they feed you first with a delicious burst of color. I just love to mix these and the bright red of the Hong Vit radish with a grated carrot for a feast of color that brings ooohs and aaahs both at home and in my classes.

Kogane

Kogane is a type of Chinese cabbage with a bright light green leaf. The shoot has a delicate, almost sweet cabbage flavor, much like the mature cabbage. It doesn't grow tall but is well worth the effort for a hint of sweet in a salad.

Chinese Cabbage

These terrific greens look like a tray of tiny bow ties. They have a strong flavor and will keep growing for up to 2 weeks. They're perfect for cutting up into a soup, adding their unusual-shaped leaves and strong flavor.

Red and Purple Cabbage

Red and purple cabbage have a flavor similar to broccoli and are fun to grow for the colorful addition they give to a salad or to use snipped as a garnish on soup or over cottage cheese. They're expensive seeds for a small harvest, but if you have some leftover from the outdoor garden, it is a treat to grow them as shoots.

that didn't involve five different trays of greens. Thus, the first combination I called the Lunch Box Mix.

The second was during my classes when folks asked how much to grow for only one person, pointing out that five trays is more than they would use in a single day or even several days. They figured they only needed 3 or 4 ounces (85.1 or 113.4 g) of greens a day, so I started by putting equal amounts of the five basic seeds into a jar and mixing them up. Growing them all together in one tray produced surprising results. The otherwise big and bold sunflower grew bashful and slow. The slow-growing broccoli shoots seemed to leap up along with fast-growing radish. It was interesting and inspiring, but most importantly *it worked*. Using the same techniques I use for the rest of the seeds got me growing salad mixes.

SEED

A tablespoon for a small tray is the right amount of seed when it includes both large and small seeds. It is pretty easy to scoop out a blend of seeds that remain relatively consistent in proportion to the blend of seeds in

The Lunch Box Mix is sunflower, daikon radish, pea, buckwheat, canola, and cress seeds. During my classes when folks once asked how much to grow for only one person, pointing out that five trays is more than they would use in one day or even several days, we figured they only needed 3 or 4 ounces (85.1 or 113.4 g) of greens a day. I put equal amounts of the five basic seeds into a jar, mixed them up, and planted them. The results were great and took care of folks who wanted a small amount of mixed greens every day.

the jar. If you get a few more pea than sunflower, it doesn't matter much at harvest time. You will always get a decent salad despite slight variation in the mix.

For me just seeing a mix of seeds in a jar brings a feeling of excitement, like a jar of magic potion, vibrant with potential. The blend of colors, shapes, and sizes is inspiring. On the practical side it's a way to grow mixed greens in one tray to take to work or use as a single serving. The size of the harvest is easy to adjust by planting a larger tray—you can double the harvest by using a large tray. For a single person one small tray of mix a day is plenty; for two people one large tray a day will do. As a bonus with mixes I sometimes add a touch of spicy greens that I find too strong to use alone, like cress and arugula, to a mix of milder greens. And it's fun to add colorful shoots like the Hong Vit to give greens extra "visual" spice.

Sow

Planting the mixes is the same as planting the large seeds: Soak 1 tablespoon (14.8 ml) for a small tray. Try to distribute the various seeds evenly. Place the seeds in a row down the middle of the tray, and then spread them across the soil with your fingers (or the back of a spoon). Using this "windrow" of seeds to start can help disperse them evenly, versus the common technique of dumping a pile of seeds in the center of the tray and pushing them around.

Grow

Wait an extra day, 5 days instead of the usual 4 days, if the shoots are not up a full inch (2.5 cm) before putting them in the light. Turn them daily when you water so they don't lean toward the light and fall over. The mixes seem to take an extra day or two; when you see the pea shoots rise above everything else, it is close to harvest time.

Harvest

Pick off the hulls of buckwheat and sunflower; then use scissors to cut about ¼ inch (0.6 cm) above the soil line. If you plan to use the sprouts later, you can store them in a plastic bag in the refrigerator. Make sure you clean them first.

Cleaning

Rinse the stem ends of the greens first; then immerse the pile of greens in a shallow tray of clean water, pushing the greens down to let the broccoli and radish hulls float off and spill over the edge.

Cook or Fresh?

The mixes are best fresh but can be used in a wilted salad or pasta salad. The Red Mix (recipe below) can only be used for fresh salads or snipped into a soup for garnish.

Troubleshooting

You will have to pull the hulls off the sunflowers during growing. They grow slowly in the mix and need help to shed their hulls.

Special Techniques

Harvesting the tray of mixed greens is a bit of a compromise. The small greens need to grow large enough to cut, but the large greens need to be small enough that they're still tender and haven't started to send out their first true leaves. When I'm spreading seeds around the tray, I try to keep the smaller seeds closer to the outside of the tray and the larger ones toward the center.

My Favorite Mixes

Lunch Box Mix

½ cup (118.4 ml) sunflower
½ cup (118.4 ml) daikon radish
½ cup (118.4 ml) pea
½ cup (118.4 ml) buckwheat
⅓ cup (78.9 ml) broccoli or canola
1 tablespoon (14.8 ml) curly cress or mustard

Mix equal parts sunflower, radish, pea, and buckwheat and a one-third portion of broccoli with just a little cress or mustard if you prefer, to add a touch of spice.

Mild Mix

1 cup (236.8 ml) buckwheat
1 cup (236.8 ml) pea

Mix equal parts buckwheat and pea. These two seem to like growing together. The peas support the buckwheat somewhat.

The Red Mix soil sprouts are an explosion of bright shades of red and pink that adds that extra something to a special meal. The whole week I think, "Just wait until they see this on their plate" as the plants mature in the sun.

Buckwheat is glad to take second fiddle and grow in the peas' shadow. Both have subtle flavors that work well together as a simple salad or the base of a salad with grated carrots and chunks of radishes and cucumber topped with your favorite dressing.

Sandwich Mix

1 cup (236.8 ml) sunflower
1 cup (236.8 ml) buckwheat

Because these two greens are very tender—tender enough to bite off—they work great in a big heaping pile on a sandwich or in a wrap. There is no need to chop these greens, just use them like a big leaf of lettuce.

Spicy Mix

1 teaspoon (4.9 ml) cress
2 teaspoons (9.8 ml) mustard
1 teaspoon (4.9 ml) arugula

Add to 2⅓ cups (552.5 ml) of Lunch Box Mix (above).

Even though they don't produce a lot of greens, cress, mustard, and arugula are so potent that a little goes a long way. In fact cress has such a strong fragrance that you can catch a hint of it while it's growing in the tray. It spices up the air as well as the salad. Be careful: These are potent greens and not for folks who shrink at the sight of a hot pepper.

Red Mix

1 teaspoon (4.9 ml) buckwheat
1 teaspoon (4.9 ml) Hong Vit radish
½ teaspoon (2.5 ml) purple kohlrabi
½ teaspoon (2.5 ml) amaranth

This is a showy mix for special occasions. To get bright colors put this tray in full sun so the buckwheat stems get deep red and pink.

Indoor Salad in a Pinch

My stepdaughter Claudia and her husband live in Prince Edward Island (PEI) in Canada every summer and in either New Mexico, Vermont, or Eleuthera for the rest of the year. They stop here in Vermont every year for a visit before heading up to the glorious beaches and quiet life of PEI. One time when Claudia and her husband Jim visited us in Vermont, it was June already and a little too late to start a regular garden, but she really had the garden bug and wanted to do something for fresh greens. I went over making outdoor garden beds and starting fast-growing short-season varieties to get something to harvest as quick as possible. I teach classes in the Square Foot Gardening method, so I gave her a quick lesson. She knew that I was growing the soil sprouts all winter, and I had a few still going for the local school and for our salads. Claudia needed a fast source of greens, so she decided to give indoor salad gardening a try while she was establishing a garden and getting settled in PEI. She took a few bags of seeds, trays, and compost so she could start just as soon as she got there. Claudia called after a week to tell me how well it was going. She was starting them in her kitchen and greening them on a railing in her screened-in porch. Apparently you cannot live in PEI in the early summer without a screened-in porch. Anyway, they went to dinner at a mutual friend's house and brought salad made from just the soil sprouts. Everyone was so impressed that she had just arrived and already had harvested a crop of greens in such a short time. Claudia was eating from her indoor salad garden for that first month while her outdoor garden was getting started, and she continued all summer. When Claudia returned to New Mexico in the fall, she continued to grow her indoor salad garden. She was definitely hooked. I suggested at the very beginning that she grow a mix of greens to make it simple for her to start; we now call it Claudia's Mix. It is just the four basic large seeds: sunflower, peas, buckwheat, and radish. Notice in the picture that she plants a large tray or two every other day for a continuous supply.

Claudia's Mix

1 cup (236.8 ml) sunflower
1 cup (236.8 ml) daikon radish
1 cup (236.8 ml) pea
1 cup (236.8 ml) buckwheat

This picture shows Claudia's Mix at different stages of growth. She plants two of the large 4 inch by 8 inch (10.2 × 20.3 cm) trays with the mix every other day. As you can see one of the trays of mature greens on the left was missing, I suspect it was in a salad bowl somewhere. This demonstrates how indoor salad gardening can be adjusted to suit individual needs. For Claudia and her husband, Jim, one of these trays a day fills the bill.

Wheatgrass or Cat Grass

SEED: Hard red winter wheat

AMOUNT: 1 to 3 tablespoons (14.8–44.4 ml) per small tray

IN THE DARK: 4 days or 1 inch (2.5 cm) high

GREEN: 3 to 6 days

YIELD: 3 to 4 ounces (85.1–113.4 g) per small tray; 1 ounce (28.4 g) of juice

COOK: Best fresh, chewed, or as juice

HARVEST: Cut with scissors ¼ inch (0.6 cm) above soil level

CLEAN: Rinse stem ends with fresh water

DESCRIPTION

Growing wheatgrass is like growing your own vitamin pill. It's a great source of chlorophyll, but it is not a salad green. There are books written just about wheatgrass and its many beneficial uses. I like to chew a handful like gum, but it's most beneficial when juiced and used for the chlorophyll-rich drink.

Although wheatgrass is not a salad green per se, it is a remarkable food. It is not for eating; a wad of grass can be chewed for its chlorophyll or a tray can be juiced, using a special juicer, to drink small amounts as a tonic.

Cats like wheatgrass, too, and many nifty kits are available for growing it—at about 500 percent more than it should cost. So save your money and just grow it yourself in a tray. Since your cat will most likely be playing with the grass, choose a heavy ceramic flat-bottomed bowl for a tray and that may keep the tray from getting upturned in the process.

For a small tray use 1 tablespoon (14.8 ml) for cat grass (wheatgrass grown for you or cat to munch) or as much as 3 tablespoons (44.4 ml) for wheatgrass that you will juice. Notice that when you first uncover the blades of grass after their 4 days in the dark, there will be droplets of dew on the yellow shoots. I haven't looked into why this happens to them and not to other sprouts, but it's like finding gems in your cupboard reminiscent of raindrops and sparkling snow. Maybe it's the kid in me, but I get a kick out of it. It's like having a summer morning in your cupboard in the dead of winter.

SEED

My first choice for wheatgrass is the hard red winter wheat. That said, almost any variety of wheat will work for wheatgrass. Rinse the dry seeds very well, and like pea seeds make sure to soak them in plenty of fresh water.

SOW

How much you plant depends on how you intend to use the grass. Sow 1 tablespoon (14.8 ml) to chew the grass and 3 tablespoons (44.4 ml) if you want to grow it to juice. If you are growing wheatgrass for your cat to nibble on in the winter, or all year long if you're living in an apartment, plant 1 tablespoon (14.8 ml) for the small tray. Spread the seeds evenly across the moist soil; if you are using 3 tablespoons (44.4 ml), the seeds will overlap, so just try for an even layer of seeds.

GROW

The wheat doesn't require the warm temperatures that the other seeds need; still, if you can place the tray in a warm place, the wheat will grow faster. The tender yellow spikes of grass will grow quickly, sending up deep green blades of grass. Wheatgrass can soak up a tremendous amount of water day to day, so stay on top of the watering for grass that is sweet and succulent whether you are using it for juicing or chewing or for your pets. You may find that you need half a cup of water daily!

HARVEST

Use scissors or a knife to cut the grass at the soil line. I like to cut in even lengths when I cut blades of grass. If you are going to chew the grass, just cut enough for the single use—about an inch (2.5 cm) of grass. Cut the whole tray for juicing.

CLEANING

A quick rinse of the stems is all you need to make sure there is no dirt left at the base of the blades of grass.

COOK OR FRESH?

Wheatgrass can only be used fresh. The fresher the better. Because cut greens start to lose nutritional value after 3 days, it's best to use them as soon as you cut them. If you don't need all of a tray at once, leave the rest until you're ready to use it and continue to water.

TROUBLESHOOTING

If you plant 3 tablespoons (44.4 ml) in a small tray, you'll have to water generously, with about ¼ to ½ cup (59.2–118.4 ml) of water daily. If the tips turn brown, then you need more daily water. After about 14 days the grass outgrows the tray, and no matter how much you water the tips will brown a little.

SPECIAL TECHNIQUES

If you are juicing the wheatgrass, feed small bundles of grass into the hopper at a time or it'll clog. If you decide to chew the grass, do not swallow the wad of grass.

GROW SEEDS

Wheat is easy to grow in a garden, but like corn it requires a lot of space. Start with a 5 foot by 10 foot (1.5 × 3 m) bed to try it out before you decide to grow a large plot. This should yield about a gallon of wheat berries, which will last about 10 months when planted for sprouts.

Mustards, Cress, and Arugula

These greens are hot and spicy, much hotter than radish. I only use them in mixes along with milder greens. We've grown many trays of these varieties at my house but found that, straight up, they're just too strong. If you can eat a jalapeño pepper with ease, then you'll do fine with these greens. For the rest of us use them in a mix.

If you're not using mustard, cress, or arugula in a mix with other seeds, you'll notice that when you soak the seeds they form a gel-like glob. I think they look like fish eggs. It was a real challenge the first time I tried to get this mass of seeds to spread out over the soil. Almost by accident I discovered that by mixing the soaked seeds with a couple of

There are tons of interesting greens you can grow with this method, and it is fun to try different greens. The garnet giant mustard pictured here has a slight dark red blush on the light green leaves; some even get dark maroon color and make an unusual addition to a salad.

tablespoons of moistened soil mix, the resulting paste was easier to spread out across the tray and they grew beautifully. It was a humorous scene with me trying to spread out the sticky seeds and getting all covered with goop like a cartoon character. I ended up scraping off all the seeds with soil stuck to them, then taking the ball of soil and seeds, flattening it out like a pancake and laying it on the soil. Presto, it worked perfectly. Still—let me warn you again—a whole tray of these spicy greens in a salad may have your stomach doing backflips like an Olympic diver, so proceed with caution!

For cress you'll probably want to plant the Persian cress or cressida curly cress. Watercress grows too slowly for our purposes. Any of the arugula or mustards work well. The garnet giant mustard has a maroon leaf that adds color to the mixture. Though they all pack a bite each of these has its own distinct flavor. The cress has a bright, sweet, spicy fragrance, too. I use 1 teaspoon (4.9 ml) of these seeds in a mixture with about 1 cup (236.8 ml) of the milder seeds. Start with that proportion and work up to more if you like it hotter. There are 16 tablespoons in a cup, so 2 tablespoons (29.6 ml) of cress seeds in a cup would be a strong mix.

Clover and Alfalfa

I was really surprised at how easy it is to grow clover and alfalfa in soil, because I had always associated them with sprouting in jars. They're much more productive when grown in soil than in jars, and the shoots have a delicate green flavor in a salad. I can't help describing the clover as looking like a flag on a golf putting green. After a few days in the sun, clover sends up a little flaglike leaf that lets you know it is ready to harvest. Try these thin and crisp soil sprouts for a different texture in your salad, and enjoy how much easier they are to grow in soil.

Popcorn Shoots

I like growing popcorn shoots mostly because they're so pretty. With bright, pale green blades and red stems, they're a great-looking houseplant. For eating, though, I like to grow them in the dark cupboard for the entire time so they blanch. Then they develop a light yellow shoot that's very sweet. Chopping a little into a salad adds that sweet touch like maple syrup in a vinaigrette and can cut the bitterness of an endive or radicchio.

Nasturtium

I first tried nasturtium seeds on a whim—I didn't think they'd work for soil sprouts at all, never, no way. To the contrary I found the young leaves are delicious—hot as all get out, but very flavorful.

Another good thing: One planting of nasturtium will last for weeks on the windowsill. Just keep clipping leaves and watering the tray and they'll keep growing. Don't expect to use nasturtium greens for the bulk of your salad, though. They're a taste treat to add to a bowl of greens, but too hot to use in great quantity.

To grow them soak about twenty of the huge seeds as usual and plant them in a small tray just like the sunflower seeds.

Amaranth Red Giant

The brilliant pink color of amaranth's stem and leaf wakes up a salad bowl with eye-popping color. The beetlike flavor makes this a peculiar taste but mixes well with other greens. It likes a high germination temperature, so make sure to put these seeds in your warmest spot. Harvest amaranth early, in about 8 days, rather than letting them go to 10 days as you would broccoli. If you leave them in the soil, they'll turn brown and die back, so once you see the seed leaf turn deep red, it's time to harvest. Amaranth is an ingredient in my Red Mix. Because it's expensive and not that productive, I use it mostly for the mix and rarely grow a whole tray.

Adzuki Bean

Adzuki is one of the few beans that grows well and produces a good-tasting shoot. The adzuki shoots are similar to pea shoots but are smaller and

The picture of red giant amaranth does not do justice to the brilliant red of the stems and leaves. It is not very tasty, I must admit, but very worth the effort for the flashy addition to a salad. It is one of the ingredients in the Red Mix listed on page 136.

Adzuki beans are a great pleasure to grow. Adzuki is one of the few types of beans that grows well in soil and that has a delicious flavor. The red of the beans is jewel-like and the broad leaf and succulent stalk is a terrific addition to a salad. They can be used as a replacement for pea shoots.

One of my students suggested the French lentils, and I am glad he did. They have a featherlike frond green, which is a nice addition to the windowsill and the salad. Like pea shoots they should be chopped into small pieces and can be used for cooking greens as well.

thinner with two large seed leaves at the top of the stalks. I use adzuki in a stir-fry with peas to add texture, and they're good in a salad, too. Plant 1 tablespoon (14.8 ml) per small tray.

French Lentils

These were recommended by one of my students. I generally shy away from beans, but French lentils, like adzuki beans, are good. I enjoy their thin stem and decorative leaf shape. You can use these shoots instead of peas in a salad or add them to a stir-fry with peas and adzuki for similar flavors and different shapes and textures. I use a heaping tablespoon (22.2 ml) of French lentils in a small tray.

Fenugreek

Fenugreek is a popular herb in Indian cuisine, used as a spice, for fresh greens or salads, and cooked with vegetables. It is easy to grow using the same techniques as described above. The greens can be bitter if you plan to use them fresh, but the bitterness is lost when they are cooked. If you don't want the bitterness, try blanching them to keep their

Onions and Garlic: Not Strictly Soil Sprouts, but Worth a Mention

Growing onions as sprouts was a mystery to me. Sprouting them in jars was an exercise in futility, yielding little, hard black seeds with a tiny white root lazily appearing after days of rinsing. I tried the same technique I use for soil sprouts, with disappointing results, and gave up even though I thought a mild onion flavor would be a nice addition to my salads. One of my garden friends mentioned that she was sprouting garlic in a pot using the small buds that form at the top of a hardneck variety. Clever, I thought, and tried it, and I was delighted that it worked well. But it did not solve my onion problem. The next summer another friend sent me a clump of walking onions, also known as Egyptian onions, potato onions, multiplier onions, and a few more names besides. They are like shallots in that they form several bulbs at the base instead of one bulb like a standard onion. But the walking onions also form a flower head of many tiny cloves at the top of the stalk. Thus the name: When the stalk falls over the bulbs form a new plant, spreading or "walking" around the garden. When I saw one of these bulbs with all those cloves, I thought about the garlic and determined to give these a try over the winter with my soil sprouts. It worked

very well, and I am pleased to say this is a great way to add fresh onion to the winter salad. The technique is the same as the soil sprouts, with slight adjustments. Instead of the shallow tray use a deep pot with a saucer. I like to use the so-called self-watering pots that have a reservoir at the bottom for water to supply a steady source of moisture. Planting is the same—you cover the whole surface of the pot with the tiny cloves, closely packed and actually touching. Once planted cover the cloves with sopping newspaper and put them in the dark for 4 days, just like the soil sprouts. When the shoots of onions push the paper up, they are ready for the light—this might be in 4 days or a little more. The other difference from the soil sprouts is that this pot will grow and regrow after harvest for several weeks of fresh onion tips for a salad. Walking onions are well worth the effort and a fun addition to the indoor garden. One hurdle you will have to jump is finding "seeds" for this. If you have your own garden, you can plant the walking onions and expect a crop of the cloves the first year. But if you don't have a garden, then the simplest solution is to buy onion sets, plant some, and store the rest in the vegetable drawer of your fridge until you need them.

sweetness and soften the bitter. To blanch them just grow them in the dark for the whole time, never putting them into the light. Blanched they are completely yellow and add a spicy exotic flavor to a salad. Well worth the effort. Soak 1 tablespoon (14.8 ml) of seeds for a small tray.

Rutabagas

Whoda thunk it? Rutabagas are great. They have tiny greens like broccoli, and you use just 1 teaspoon (4.9 ml) of seeds for a small tray. The flavor is spicier than broccoli, and you might want to consider using rutabaga seeds in a mix of other small seeds—for instance canola, purple kolhrabi, and Chinese cabbage—adding a little spice to their mild sweet flavors. Grown all together they make an interesting salad mix for variety. Four trays of these mixed together make a fairly small salad, so you might want to pair these with a meal that would work well with a smaller side dish of greens.

Turnips

Turnips are similar to rutabagas with a spicy flavor. They are mild enough, however, to add a whole small tray to a salad. Why would you choose to grow turnip soil sprouts? There are a few good reasons. First because the greens are different enough in taste, color, and texture to make for a nice change. Also because I grow turnips in my outdoor earth garden, I have seeds leftover every season. It is such a great way to use up the extra seeds. A mere teaspoon (4.9 ml) of seeds for a small tray should yield about an ounce of delicious greens.

Pac Choi and Red Pac Choi

Pac choi and red pac choi are grown like broccoli: 1 teaspoon (4.9 ml) of seeds for a small tray. I usually choose the red variety because the maroon blush on the large leaves adds a nice change of texture to the usual canola that I grow on a regular basis. One advantage to growing red pac choi is that like all of the cole family, they will grow for a few weeks before the true leave appears. That means you can grow several trays and use them as you need them without worrying about them overgrowing to the point where they are no longer usable.

Magenta Spreen (Lambsquarters)

Magenta spreen is a cousin to the common weed lambsquarters. The leaves of the mature plant have a red-magenta blush on the leaves that is pretty, and they taste like spinach. These tiny soil sprout greens have an exotic flavor, not quite like spinach, that offers another nice change in flavor and texture. They are small seeds, so plant them the same as broccoli, 1 teaspoon (4.9 ml) of seeds per small tray. Because spinach is not a good choice for soil sprouts, try magenta spreen for a change that is somewhat like spinach. Also try magenta spreen if you really like eating lambsquarters.

Dark Purple and Green Mizuna

Dark purple mizuna has a slightly larger seed leaf, so it is a better choice for soil sprouts, but it also costs twice as much, and this might discourage you from trying it. The green mizuna has pretty heart-shaped leaves and the same sweet flavor that is a characteristic of the cole family. Again, planting mizuna is a great way to use up leftover outdoor garden seeds.

Tatsoi

We grow a lot of tatsoi in our outdoor earth garden as an important ingredient for kimchi. This means we have leftover seeds every year. It is a great soil sprout with a hot flavor that is slightly bitter, and it has a dark leaf like the mature vegetable. One teaspoon (4.9 ml) for the small tray is plenty of seeds for a nice full head of greens.

Red Russian Kale

Red Russian kale has a mild kale flavor with a pretty pale purple stem, similar to the purple kohlrabi soil sprouts. It is a fun addition to a salad to contrast with the other greens. There is something about the orange of grated carrot with the pale purple of these stems that gives your senses a wake-up call in the winter. The flavor is a hint of sweet and the deep green of kale. It would be enough to have wonderful flavor, but these greens also have the same nutrient-dense characteristic of broccoli and all of the cole family of greens, a real bonus any time of year.

Collards

Another packet of seeds that I regularly have left over from outdoor gardening is collards, and they make good soil sprouts. They have a similar flavor and texture to kale. At the end of the outdoor garden season, I line up packets of seeds that I know I can use for soil sprouts through the winter months and include the collards. It is such a great feeling—like cordwood in the woodshed; I am ready to face the long, cold winter because I get to garden the whole time. Plant 1 teaspoon (4.9 ml) of seeds in a small tray. Like broccoli they may take more than 4 days in the dark if it is cool in the cupboard, so wait until they are up 1 inch (2.5 cm) before putting them on the windowsill. Your patience will be repaid with long silvery stems and a nice head of greens for your salad bowl.

Tendril Peas

Tendril peas are grown the same way as pea shoots: 1 tablespoon (14.8 ml) for the small tray. They are different from snow peas in that they produce tiny tendrils very low on the shoots, and the shoot has a lot of these tendrils along with the leaves. The taste is identical to regular pea shoots, but they have the extra texture of the tendrils. They are nice for a variation and look enticing on a plate alone with the Red Currant Vinaigrette (see Red Mix Salad on page 153).

Purple Radish

Purple radish are grown just like daikon radish using 1 tablespoon (14.8 ml) of seeds for a small tray. The flavor is not as hot as daikon radish, and the main drawback is that the dark purple leaves look black in a salad when you put salad dressing over the greens. Used in a special recipe with a dressing that does not have oil, the purple won't turn black. Just another option for fun. They can be hard to find, but if you can find them at a reasonable price, they are another options for your indoor salad garden.

CHAPTER 16

Recipes

All-Star-All-Sprout Salad

When I first started experimenting with soil sprout salads, this was the one that everyone loved and asked for over and over. It quickly became a family all-star. It's also the salad I usually serve at the end of each soil sprout class. Some folks in classes take their salad eating very seriously and make a point of trying the salad without dressing first. This salad gets rave reviews every time I serve it, no matter whether it is dressed or not; I hope you enjoy it as well.

1 cup (236.8 ml) chopped
    sunflower greens
1 cup (236.8 ml) chopped pea shoots
1 cup (236.8 ml) chopped
    radish greens
1 cup (236.8 ml) chopped
    buckwheat lettuce
½ cup (118.4 ml) chopped
    broccoli greens
2 tablespoons (29.6 ml) sunflower oil
2 tablespoons (29.6 ml)
    balsamic vinegar
Herb salt to taste

Mix the chopped greens in a bowl with the herb salt. Add oil and vinegar and toss. I know it sounds too simple, but trust me this is one of the best; give it a try at least once. If you are not sure that you're going to finish the salad, just mix half greens with half the dressing because the salad won't keep that well if it has dressing on the greens.

Variation: Add 2 peeled and grated carrots to add a contrasting color and body to the salad. Any salad is enhanced with one ripe avocado, peeled and diced.

Yield: 4 servings

Mike's Own Mother's Day Salad

My oldest son Mike came to visit for Mother's Day and put this salad together. It became an instant favorite. This is perfect for early spring because I am still growing pea shoots and radish greens indoors and winter spinach and leaf lettuce are starting to produce outdoors.

2 cups (473.6 ml) (about 2 small trays) radish greens that have been cut ½ inch long

2 cups (473.6 ml) (about 2 small trays) chopped pea shoots

2 cups (473.6 ml) fresh spinach leaves

4 leaves romaine lettuce

¼ cup (59.2 ml) walnut pieces, lightly roasted

¼ cup (59.2 ml) grated parmesan cheese

3 tablespoons (44.4 ml) virgin olive oil

1 tablespoon (14.8 ml) balsamic vinegar

1 teaspoon (4.9 ml) salt or herb salt, such as Spike

Chop the greens and lettuce into ½ inch pieces. Tear the spinach leaves. Roast the walnut pieces in a cast-iron skillet over very low heat for 5 minutes. Stir frequently, about every 30 seconds, making sure each piece is turned. Meanwhile toss the greens in a salad bowl with the salt.

Just before serving add the oil and vinegar and toss. Sprinkle with roasted walnuts.

Variations: Substitute Hong Vit radish for the regular radish. Roast walnuts in maple syrup or soy sauce with a tablespoon of butter.

Yield: 6 servings

Lunchbox Salad

Inspired by my wife's request to grow a whole salad in one tray, I mixed the five basic seeds—sunflower, pea, radish, buckwheat, and canola (what I call the poor man's broccoli)—in a tray. To give the mix a little pizzazz, I added mustard, cress, Hong Vit radish, and purple kohlrabi. This made a feast for the eyes as well as the palate.

4 cups (947.2 ml) chopped mixed greens from 2 large trays (4 × 8 inch / 10.2 × 20.3 cm)

2 carrots, peeled and grated

8 ounces feta cheese, crumbled

DRESSING:

Juice of 1 lime

3 tablespoons (44.4 ml) olive oil

¼ cup (59.2 ml) fresh chopped basil leaves

Chop the mixed greens into ¼-inch (0.6 cm) pieces, add the carrots and feta cheese, top with dressing, mix, and serve. The feta cheese is salty, so sample the salad before you add more salt.

Yield: 4 servings

Sam's Wilted Sunflower-Kale Salad

My stepdaughter Samantha and I enjoy trading recipes. This one is a jewel. I would normally say that it does not store well, but in fact that has never been a problem—the bowl is always empty by the end of a meal.

2 cups (473.6 ml) chopped kale

2 cups (473.6 ml) (about 2 small trays) chopped sunflower greens

½ red onion, sliced extremely thin and chopped into 1-inch (2.5 cm) lengths

½ cup (118.4 ml) raw cashews, chopped

¾ cup (177.6 ml) pineapple chunks in light syrup

¾ cup (177.6 ml) manchego cheese, shaved

Dressing:

Juice of 1 lemon

2 cloves of garlic, pressed or diced fine

½ cup (118.4 ml) olive oil

Salt and pepper to taste (my suggestion is to go heavy on the pepper)

Mix the dressing first and let it set while you make the salad. Steam the kale until it's tender. (It takes a while to make kale tender! Could be 10 minutes.)

Chop the sunflower greens longer than usual, about 1 inch (2.5 cm).

Mix the onions, pineapple, and sunflower greens. Drain excess water off the kale and mix it into the other ingredients while it is still warm enough to wilt the sunflower greens. Just before serving add the dressing, cashews, and cheese, and toss.

Variations: Use pine nuts instead of cashews. Use fresh spinach instead of kale, and warm the salad dressing to pour over the salad and wilt the greens. Use asiago cheese in place of manchego cheese.

Yield: 4 Servings

This is our everyday salad. It has the five basic greens: sunflower, radish (in this case the purple-stemmed Hong Vit radish), buckwheat, pea shoots, and canola, with grated carrot mixed in for added color. I serve this at the end of every class, and it always gets rave reviews.

Radish Relish

This is a cooling summer dip for raw veggies, chips, or a sauce over cooked vegetables. The yogurt softens the heat of the greens, and you're left with the radish and dill flavors.

2 trays daikon radish greens, chopped
¼ cup (59.2 ml) plain yogurt
1 teaspoon (4.9 ml) dried dill weed
   (or 1 tablespoon [14.8 ml] fresh,
   if possible)
1 teaspoon (4.9 ml) rice vinegar
1 teaspoon (4.9 ml) salt

Chop the radish greens very fine, about ⅛ inch long. In a bowl mix the greens with yogurt, dill, vinegar, and salt. Turn the ingredients a few times, and then refrigerate to give the flavors a chance to permeate the mix.

Be sure to remove the dish from the fridge about an hour before the meal so the greens have a chance to come to room temperature before serving.

Variations: Use Hong Vit radish or purple radish for a more colorful dip. Add a table-spoon of horseradish for eye-popping flavor. Might just bring a tear to your eye!

Yield: 4 small servings

Rice Salad

This was one of those pleasant surprises that started when I mixed the salad and rice on my plate. It was so good that I decided to make it as a prepared dish. It is a great way to add a serving of veggies to a really quick meal with leftover rice.

4 cups (947.2 ml) cooked basmati rice
   (leftover rice works well)
4 tablespoons (59.2 ml) soy sauce
2 tablespoons (29.6 ml) olive oil
Prepared All-Star-All-Sprout Salad

In a large cast-iron skillet over high heat, stir-fry rice in oil, turning constantly for 5 minutes or until the rice is evenly heated. Add the soy sauce and continue stirring for another minute.

Transfer the rice to a mixing bowl. Add the salad with the dressing on it to the rice and mix together.

Serve in rice bowls.

Variations: Stir-fry seitan pieces over high heat until browned. Add to the rice before mixing with salad. Substitute pasta noodles for rice.

Yield: 6 servings

Red Mix Salad

This salad is eye candy. The Red Mix on page 136 develops bright red, purple, and pink stems and deep green leaves. When you are looking for a special treat or a midwinter pick-me-up, try this salad with Red Currant Vinaigrette. It's a favorite at our house. Again I have to thank my daughter Sam for the inspiration for the dressing, another regular request in our family. Bon appétit!

2–3 cups (473.6–710.4 ml) chopped
   Red Mix (4 small trays)

RED CURRANT
VINAIGRETTE DRESSING:

2 tablespoons (29.6 ml) red currant
   jam or jelly
1 tablespoon (14.8 ml) Worcestershire
   sauce (I use Annie's Vegan)
2 tablespoons (29.6 ml) of
   balsamic vinegar
1 tablespoon (14.8 ml) dijon mustard
1 teaspoon (4.9 ml) tamari
2 teaspoons (9.8 ml) maple syrup
   (the real stuff)
1 teaspoon (4.9 ml) kosher salt
½ teaspoon (2.5 ml) herb salt,
   such as Spike
1 cup (236.8 ml) sunflower oil
2 cloves crushed garlic

Cut, wash, and chop the Red Mix, and make sure all of the hulls from the buckwheat lettuce are picked off the greens. Chop the greens fine, about ⅛-inch (0.3 cm) lengths at the stem ends and ¼-inch (0.6 cm) lengths for the leaf. Mix the dressing ingredients in a 1-pint (59.2 ml) canning jar with a lid. Cover the jar tightly and shake for a minute. Dress the greens and enjoy. That's all there is to it.

Variations: Add chopped red cabbage, apple, and candied pecans to the Red Mix. Add grated beets and finely chopped red onion to the Red Mix.

Yield: 4 servings

Like a pasta salad this combination of rice with dressed All-Star-All-Sprout Salad is a great one-dish dinner or a contribution to a summer potluck. The trick is adding the salad as the very last step so the greens are only wilted by the hot rice and not really cooked.

Tempura

Tempura is Japanese-style deep-fried vegetables. Our family indulges in it for dinner once in a while, as a special treat. Tempura takes time to prepare and cook, but it is well worth the trouble. We batter and fry onions, squash, kale, zucchini, asparagus, and about any garden veggie we may have around. We've added soil sprouts to this list and been delighted with the results. When you're in the mood to indulge, batter-fried soil sprouts are a wonderful, crisp, and delicate addition to any meal.

BATTER:

2 cups (472.6 ml) white all-purpose flour
¾ cup (177.6 ml) arrowroot starch
2–3 cups (473.6–710.4 ml) ice water or cold beer

VEGETABLES:

2 cups (473.6 ml) chopped pea shoots, cut into 1-inch (2.5 cm) lengths
2 cups (473.6 ml) chopped broccoli soil sprouts, cut into 1-inch (2.5 cm) lengths
1 cup (236.8 ml) carrots, sliced into ¼-inch (0.6 cm) pieces and steamed 3 minutes
1 cup (236.8 ml) broccoli florets, cut into 1-inch (2.5 cm) heads and steamed 3 minutes
1 cup (236.8 ml) chopped zucchini, cut into ¼-inch (0.6 cm) slices
1 cup (236.8 ml) chopped onion, cut into ¼-inch (0.6 cm) slices
4 cups (947.2 ml) cooking oil (many folks prefer peanut oil for deep frying)

DIPPING SAUCE:

¼ cup (59.2 ml) soy sauce
1 tablespoon (14.8 ml) grated ginger
1 tablespoon (14.8 ml) maple syrup
3 cloves garlic, crushed

In a medium-sized bowl add cold water or beer to flour and stir to pancake-batter consistency. Don't overmix. Batter can be a little lumpy. Place the bowl of batter into a larger bowl of ice water to keep the mixture cold.

When the batter is mixed and vegetables are cut and ready to dip, heat 2 inches (5.1 cm) of oil in a cast-iron skillet (or use a deep fryer on a French fry setting). To test that the oil is at the right temperature, drop a dollop of batter into the pan. The batter should sink to the bottom then come back up again. If it only sinks, the oil is too cold. If it rises quickly or does not sink at all, the batter is too hot.

Have a rack ready to drain your deep-fried veggies and shoots.

Make thin patties out of the cut shoots, scooping a tablespoonful at a time. Drop the patty into the batter, then transfer to the hot oil. The patties will drop to the bottom of the skillet then rise to the top of the oil. Fry until light brown. Remove from oil and drain on a cooling rack. It takes a while to fry up enough for a meal, so we transfer the fried and drained patties to a large pan kept in a warm oven.

Dip cut veggies in batter and then drop in hot oil. Fry until light brown.

In a separate bowl combine ingredients for dipping sauce. Serve with tempura vegetables.

Yield: 4 servings

Garlic Pea Shoots

The inspiration for this recipe was my Chinese friend who cooked potato and jalapeño peppers for my wife and me during a visit to our home. We got to talking about the pea shoots over this meal, and he told me how his mom cooked them. This is a simplified version.

4 cups (947.2 ml) chopped pea shoots
   cut in ¼-inch (0.6 cm) lengths
4 garlic cloves, slivered
1 onion, chopped
1 cup (236.8 ml) sliced mushrooms
1 teaspoon (4.9 ml) grated ginger
1 tablespoon (14.8 ml) water or
   vegetable broth

Sauté onions, garlic, and mushrooms over low heat (to draw out the juices) until the onions are clear. Add ginger and the broth or water; stir for a minute, then add chopped pea shoots; cover and remove from heat. Serve within 5 minutes, while the shoots are bright green.

Variations: Add whole peas to the sautéed vegetables. Crush two more cloves of garlic at the end and stir into the cooked vegetables just before adding the pea shoots.

Yield: 4 servings

Peppered Turkey Sandwich

Peppered turkey was always a favorite sandwich meat before I decided to follow a vegetarian diet, and lucky for me there are really good wholesome vegetarian sliced "meats" that I can use for sandwiches. I use the whole sunflower soil sprouts in a great big heap to top off this great-tasting sandwich.

4 slices soft, full-bodied white bread
2 tablespoons (29.6 ml) mayonnaise
2 tablespoons (29.6 ml) mustard
4 slices peppered turkey
2 slices provolone cheese
2 slices red onion, thinly sliced
Sliced green pepper, to taste
2 slices ripe tomato
Handful of sunflower greens, whole,
   not chopped

Spread mayo on one slice of bread and mustard on the other. Fold the turkey slices and place them on one slice of bread, then add the tomato, green pepper, and onion. Arrange the greens so the stems are pointing toward the middle and the green leaves line the edges of the bread.

With each bite you get crisp green leaves. If you add sliced avocado, you'll be heaven bound!

Hummus Wrap

Soil sprouts are a natural for wraps. You can put a huge pile of greens on top of all the fixings and still fold it up. Buckwheat or sunflower greens are great because they're so tender and easy to bite into, like lettuce leaves. I am offering one of my favorites, but there are lots of great variations on the theme.

1 soft wheat tortilla

2 tablespoons (29.6 ml) garlic hummus

2 slices provolone cheese

2 tablespoons (29.6 ml) salsa or diced tomato

2 ounces (56.7 g) buckwheat sprouts, whole, not chopped (about one small tray)

Spread hummus on the tortilla. Fold provolone cheese and lay in the middle of the tortilla. Spoon salsa over the cheese. Lay buckwheat sprouts in the middle with the green leaves at the top. Fold the bottom edge up about 1 inch (2.5 cm), fold one side over the center, then roll up toward the other side. By folding the bottom edge up and rolling it tight, nothing should drip out the bottom, but better have a napkin handy even so!

Adding soil sprouts to a sandwich is a perfect replacement for lettuce. This bean taco is an example of how we make the substitution. I like the tender sunflower greens and buckwheat lettuce; they do not need to be chopped. Pea shoots should be chopped into small pieces and not used whole. Radishes are a spicy addition to a sandwich.

The following five recipes are from the recipe book of Dr. Claudia Welch, my stepdaughter, and are reprinted here with her permission. Her groundbreaking book, *Balance Your Hormones, Balance Your Life* (2011, Da Capo Press), is a great resource for women. Claudia also teaches online courses that are available at www.DrClaudiaWelch.com.

Grated Carrot and Sprout Salad

1 tablespoon (14.8 ml) freshly
  squeezed lemon juice
6 tablespoons (88.8 ml) extra virgin
  olive oil
¼ teaspoon (1.2 ml) salt
¼ teaspoon (1.2 ml) freshly
  ground pepper
½ teaspoon (2.5 ml) paprika
3 large round carrots, peeled
  and grated
1 cup (236.8 ml) chopped pea shoots
½ cup (118.4 ml) chopped parsley
¼ cup (59.2 ml) raisins
¼ cup (59.2 ml) chopped walnuts
  or pecans

Whisk together lemon juice, salt, pepper, paprika, and oil. Toss with carrots, sprouts, and parsley in a large bowl. Taste and adjust salt. Let sit 10 to 30 minutes before serving.

Variations: I like to add some kind of pickle to this—dice a big dill pickle into ¼-inch (0.6 cm) pieces. Even (believe it or not) adding sauerkraut is really good.

Yield: 4 servings

Quinoa, Sweet Pea Sprouts, and Veggies

Sprouts add a little crunch to this otherwise soft dish, as well as some vibrant color. You can use any sprouts, but I prefer the texture and density of the sweet pea.

4 tablespoons (59.2 ml) olive oil
1 medium onion, diced
2 stalks of celery, diced
2 medium to large carrots, diced
1 teaspoon (4.9 ml) salt
½ teaspoon (2.5 ml) ground pepper
½ teaspoon (2.5 ml) paprika
1 cup (236.8 ml) rinsed and
   drained quinoa
2 cups (473.6 ml) water
1 small tray chopped sweet pea sprouts

Sauté onions, carrots, and celery in oil until onions are transparent. Rinse the quinoa in a strainer. Add salt, pepper, paprika, and quinoa to the onions and veggies and sauté another few minutes, stirring until the veggies start to stick to the pan. Add water.

Bring to a boil. Turn down heat and simmer until done, about 20 minutes.

Fold in the sprouts and serve immediately.

Yield: 4 servings

It is a great treat to have dinner at Claudia's house because I get remarkable dishes like the Agni Soup that come from her Ayurveda training. Her recipes are a hybrid— part gourmet and part herbalist healer, which is a very satisfying combination. Enjoy.

Agni Soup

I like this soup during cold and flu season. It never fails to make me feel better when I think I'm coming down with something in winter.

3–4 tablespoons (44.4–59.2 ml) sunflower or safflower oil

1 tablespoon (14.8 ml) toasted sesame oil

1 onion, diced small

2 medium carrots, grated

½ cup chopped (118.4 ml) celery, sliced paper thin

½ medium daikon radish, grated (optional)

3–4 shitake mushrooms, sliced thin (rehydrate if they start out dry) (optional)

2–3 tablespoons (29.6–44.4 ml) finely grated fresh ginger

½ teaspoon (2.5 ml) ground black pepper

½ cup (118.4 ml) dulse seaweed, rinsed

1 cup (236.8 ml) thin rice noodles

2–3 tablespoons (29.6–44.4 ml) rice vinegar

1 tablespoon (14.8 ml) kudzu (dissolved first in a few tablespoons of cold water)

2 tablespoons (29.6 ml) 100 percent maple syrup

2–3 tablespoons (29.6–44.4 ml) soy sauce or tamari

1 bunch scallions, finely chopped

1 big (4 × 8 inch / 10.2 × 20.3 cm) tray radish sprouts, chopped

1–2 tablespoons (14.8–29.6 ml) miso

In a skillet sauté the onions in oil. When the onions are translucent add the carrots and celery. Sauté another minute and add the grated daikon radish and mushrooms. Sauté another minute and add the ginger, black pepper, and seaweed. Cover with about 1 to 2 inches (2.5–5.1 cm) of water.

Simmer until veggies are cooked through. Add enough water to cover the veggies, plus another 2 to 3 inches (5.1–7.6 cm). Bring to a boil and add rice noodles, rice vinegar, kudzu, maple syrup, and soy sauce or tamari. Cook until noodles are tender.

Remove from heat and add scallions, radish sprouts, and miso. (Don't boil this after you add the miso. Miso should never be boiled, or the healthy bacteria is killed.)

Bon appétit.

Yield: 4 servings

Dal with Sprouts

I find this dish is exceptionally easy to digest, even for people who have trouble digesting beans. It's nourishing by itself as a soup or over rice with a side dish of vegetables.

1 cup (236.8 ml) dry dal beans, rinsed, soaked, and drained (I prefer Toor dal, but split mung beans work fine, too)

½ cup (118.4 ml) ghee, divided

½ teaspoon (2.5 ml) brown mustard seeds

½ teaspoon (2.5 ml) cumin seeds

1 medium to large onion, diced

1 teaspoon (4.9 ml) turmeric powder or 2 teaspoons (9.8 ml) fresh, finely grated turmeric root

1 tablespoon (14.8 ml) fresh, finely grated gingerroot

1 teaspoon (4.9 ml) cumin powder

1 tablespoon (14.8 ml) coriander powder

3 cups (710.4 ml) water (a little more or less depending on how thick you want the dal to come out)

1–2 cups (236.8–473.6 ml) sprouts (I like buckwheat, pea shoots, or sunflower sprouts best because they are big enough to hold their own in the hot dal)

Salt, to taste

Place dal beans in a shallow bowl and rinse with cool water until water becomes clear. Allow beans to soak for an hour if you have the time.

Heat ¼ cup (59.2 ml) of ghee over medium heat. Ghee burns easily, so avoid high heat and don't leave it on too long. Add mustard and cumin seeds and stir until the seeds pop. Add diced onion and sauté until translucent. Add the turmeric and ginger and sauté another minute while stirring. Add rinsed and drained dal (soaked, if you had the time). Stir until the dal starts to stick. Add cumin powder, coriander powder, and water and stir, making sure to loosen dal that sticks to the bottom of the pot (or it will burn there).

Cook thoroughly until beans and ingredients are soft. Remove from heat and add the remaining ghee and salt. Fold in the sprouts. The dal is hot enough to cook the sprouts.

Serve immediately.

Yield: 4 servings

Walking into the kitchen when this is cooking is like being transported to India. I feel like a cartoon character traveling on waves of its exotic fragrance. I prefer it over rice, and the nutrient-rich soil sprouts add another dimension to the food value. Great dish.

Soil sprout salads are just a beginning to many delicious combinations like the chickpeas, red onions, and tomato pictured here. We add avocado, homemade croutons, crumbled blue cheese, and anything that we might fancy for salads.

Soba Noodles, Sprouts, and Veggies

Soba does not keep well for leftovers. It gets soggy. It's a good idea to make just enough for one meal. If you have some left over—quick get your neighbors over to finish it off.

SOBA INGREDIENTS:

Buckwheat soba (a handful does well for 2 hungry people)

2–3 tablespoons (29.6–44.4 ml) toasted sesame oil, enough to coat the cooked, drained soba

1 tablespoon (14.8 ml) soy sauce, or to taste

1 teaspoon (4.9 ml) freshly grated ginger juice, or to taste

VEGGIE INGREDIENTS:

2–3 tablespoons (29.6–44.4 ml) toasted sesame oil (enough to generously cover the bottom of the pan)

1–2 tablespoons (14.8–29.6 ml) soy sauce, to taste

1–3 teaspoons (14.8–44.4 ml) freshly grated ginger juice, to taste

1 tablespoon (14.8 ml) rice vinegar, to taste

½ teaspoon (2.5 ml) ground black pepper, to taste

½ small purple cabbage, very thinly sliced

½ cup (118.4 ml) thinly sliced shitake mushrooms

½–1 cup (118.4–236.8 ml) finely chopped kale

¼ cup (59.2 ml) hijiki seaweed (optional)

½–1 cup (118.4–236.8 ml) freshly grated carrots

½–1 cup (118.4–236.8 ml) chopped fresh sprouts of your choice (I like radish best for this, but any of them are good)

½ cup (118.4 ml) chopped scallions

3 tablespoons (44.4 ml) sesame seeds

Grate the ginger on a fine grater, and then squeeze the fresh juice and set aside.

Cook the soba according to directions on the package. Be careful not to overcook or it will become gluey. Drain. Mix in ginger juice and remaining ingredients. Serve as a base for veggie mix.

Grate the ginger on a fine grater, and then squeeze the fresh juice and set aside.

Soak hijiki seaweed for 10 minutes in cool water. Drain and set aside (if you don't like seaweed, omit this).

In a skillet sauté cabbage and mushrooms in oil over medium heat. When cabbage is almost done add kale, seaweed, soy sauce, rice vinegar, pepper, and ginger juice.

When the kale softens add carrots. When the carrots are cooked through, remove pan from heat and mix in sprouts, scallions, and sesame seeds.

Serve immediately over the soba mixture.

Yield: 4 servings

CHAPTER 17

A Final Word about Farming

I t might seem like a stretch to call growing soil sprouts in small trays "farming," but it is that in a very real way. The fact that I grow a large harvest of greens for sale qualifies as more than just gardening. My approach, though, has grown out of the same small-scale gardening practices I use for home harvest.

Dare to Think Small

I started farming by accident. Two science teachers from a local high school came to one of my evening classes. One of them had taught two of my sons, and the other was her colleague. They were interested in these techniques for themselves as gardeners at home, but as teachers they

Farming with soil sprouts starts the same as indoor salad gardening: You soak the seeds, in this case using about twenty-five small glass or plastic cups with 2 tablespoons (29.6 ml) of dry seeds in each. Twenty-five of the large trays, 4 inches by 8 inches (10.2 × 20.3 cm), of pea shoots will yield about 6 pounds (2.7 kg) of greens.

were curious about using soil sprout techniques in their classes. I've come to accept this as a common, almost predictable, response from teachers. Once they understand indoor salad gardening, they see its use in their classes.

One teacher was developing a program to grow greenhouse vegetables for the school cafeteria food service as part of his class curriculum. Both teachers thought that their school's food service director could grow shoots for the cafeteria's salad bar. And that I should show him how to do it!

I remember the day I stopped by to speak with the food service director; we had arranged an early morning appointment, and I brought bags of several different greens with me. I think I brought a container of mixed salad all cut up and ready to add salad dressing for him to try.

Of course seeing bags of fresh garden greens in December gets everyone excited, particularly when everything they're buying is shipped from California or somewhere else far away. The director was polite and liked what I showed him, but he said flatly, "I have no time to do this. In fact I'm short two people this morning. If you're not doing anything today, I can hire you as a temp for the day." He added, "If you grow the greens, I'll buy them. It is hard to find good greens in the winter."

And that's how I started farming shoots.

We agreed on a price for the greens based on current market values. At the time greens were sold in 3-ounce (85.1 g) bags for $3.99. That amounts to $1.33 an ounce or $20.29 a pound. I told him we would start at $1.00 an ounce and see how it went; he was happy with the arrangement.

With that decided I launched into figuring out *how* to actually do the farming part of the deal. We had agreed that we'd start with 48 ounces, or 3 pounds (1.4 kg), of greens per week and we'd adjust the amount according to the school's schedule—easy to do with shoots that have such a short growing season.

I knew that colorful sprouts would be popular on the salad bar and would probably get kids excited about their local produce, so I made sure to include Hong Vit radish for their bright red stems and deep green leaves, purple kohlrabi with beautiful violet stems, as well as the usual greens. Pea shoots, sunflower greens, and buckwheat lettuce made up the bulk of sprouts I delivered. They proved to be very popular, and we ended up growing greens right up to the end of the school year in June and started up again the next September.

Farming for the school was a great learning experience that opened my eyes to a viable home-based business that required very little to start up and had a grateful and willing customer base right within my community. Beautiful greens like this are not easy to find and harder still to ship long distances, so they are enticing for small local deli shops and restaurants, or even, as in my case, institutions like a school.

No Tractor, No Gas, No Electric Lights: How to Set Up a Small Soil Sprout Farm

The great thing about this enterprise, besides the extra $196.00 a month I was getting just from that one school, was that I didn't need to invest in lights or a greenhouse or other specialized equipment. I didn't need a plastic hoop house or a cold frame. And I didn't need a hydroponics setup. Best of all I needed no tractor or gasoline to run it.

Soil sprout farming is a very low-impact, sustainable farm model. Every week for this one customer I planted twelve of my large 4 inch by 8 inch (10.2 × 20.3 cm) trays (five sunflower, three pea, two buckwheat, one Hong Vit radish, and one purple kohlrabi), to produce 3 pounds (1.4 kg) of greens. These were the same large trays I used for my home garden. I grew them in exactly the same way.

You might wonder why I'd choose to plant five trays of sunflower when I could grow one larger tray, 10 inches by 20 inches (25.4 × 50.8 cm), for the "farm." First of all it's easier to handle a 4 inch by 8 inch tray, and I get a better crop from this size tray with no trouble from mold. It easier to check the moisture in this size tray to make sure it is evenly moist and not too wet. Plus, I get plenty of light on the windowsill. By using a windowsill instead of an electric light, the soil sprouts are grown with a smaller carbon footprint and without the additional expense for electricity. Finally growing in these smaller trays makes it easy to offer a variety of greens customized to each individual order, rather than growing a huge tray of a single variety and hoping that someone buys them all. For instance if one customer wants all pea shoots, sunflower greens, and broccoli, and another wants Hong Vit radish, buckwheat, and purple kohlrabi, I can plant for that customer exactly and plan to have the greens ready for him on the days that he wants them. Once I get to twenty-five trays I know I am at my limit. I don't promise to grow more than I have space to accommodate.

This is just the way I think and plan; if you think it would be easier for you to plant in a larger tray, like the industry standard tray, 10 inches by 20 inches (25.4 × 50.8 cm), then by all means go ahead. That size will work just fine. I know some growers who use bread trays that are 24 inches by 30 inches (61 × 76.2 cm) and some who use cafeteria trays that are 10 inches by 14 inches (25.4 × 35.6 cm). There are two things to consider. First will you have space for them in a dark place as well as by a window? And second even with a big window you may have to turn the trays midday so the greens do not lean too much. Just don't skip the 4 days in the dark!

The most common problem that I have seen with commercial growers is that they skip that first step—the easiest "do nothing" step where the trays of seeds germinate for 4 days in the dark. I was just recently at an all-day seminar presented by a market gardener, who showed one of his photos depicting this very problem—there were no stems on his sunflower greens. If you do use bigger trays, it may become a matter of logistics. When you have everything set up with shelves and lights, or shelves in a greenhouse, it seems like a lot more work to make a dark place to germinate the seeds on those big trays.

Forcing the greens to stretch in those first 4 days makes the stems longer. Longer stems means your tray is more productive. Longer stems make the greens easier to cut when you harvest the greens. The stems are crunchy and delicious just like the seed leaves. And longer stems make it easier to keep the finished greens looking clean and fresh in the bag when you present it to your customer. Don't skip this step. As you consider setting up your home for an indoor farm, keep in mind where you are going to put the trays for their incubation period.

Without changing anything in my house, I have the capacity to plant one hundred of the 4 inch by 8 inch (10.2 × 20.3 cm) trays and keep them in a dark place. I have room to green seventy-five trays in front of my

After 4 days in the dark the greens on this bookcase are ready for the sun. In a rotation between the dark cupboard and a sunlit shelf, my simple farm could produce 6 pounds (2.7 kg) a day.

windows at one time. That yields about twenty-five trays ready to harvest every day, or about 100 ounces (2.8 kg) of fresh greens daily (that translates to about 6 pounds a day, about 40 pounds [18.1 kg] each week).

The annual harvest from a farm this size would be 36,000 ounces (about 2,100 pounds, or 951.3 kg), from which I can expect gross revenues of $1.00 an ounce, and maybe more at today's prices. The $36,000 gross is not bad for a home business that fits into a typical house and requires only a modest investment in seeds, trays, and shelves. The soil can be reused and revitalized by composting the sprout roots—the soil cakes, as I call them—which are among the best fertilizers you can ask for to enrich the growing medium.

I've been known to say it often: My greenhouse is a house full of greens. In this case my farm is a house full of greens, too.

The Organization Factor

To pull this off—a farm in your house, that is—requires some organization. Taking clues from my indoor salad garden, instead of using the cupboard over the refrigerator, I placed four bookshelves with doors downstairs near the woodstove. The doors provide that added measure of darkness that helps force the young plants and encourages long stems. Remember that these long stems help to generate a more productive harvest (more ounces per tray), make it easier to cut the greens at harvest time, and add great texture to a salad. In every respect it's worth creating a dark place for the first stage—the incubation period for shoots.

Along the same line, instead of using windowsills for greening the young shoots, as in my home garden, I set up several wide shelves—each about 6 feet (182.9 cm) long—in front of the windows in my mudroom. It's where I always start my outdoor garden sets, but for shoots I don't need a south-facing window; any window will work just as well. Let me emphasize this: Any window will work just fine for soil sprouts; you do not need a bright sunny window.

I keep a calendar marked with delivery dates, count back ten to twelve days, and mark my planting dates. (I go to eleven to thirteen days when outdoor temps drop to the single digits.) I know that my maximum volume is twenty-five trays a day, so I can create a delivery schedule using this as a starting point to plan how many trays I need to plant and harvest on any given day. When I get to twenty-five trays a day, I know I'm maxed out and would have to add more shelves, more window space, and so on, to increase the capacity of my farm. The number of trays is a very precise governor of my farming operation.

If you decide that you want to try soil sprout and shoot farming, I'll pass on a few pieces of advice, knowing full well you will customize your farm to suit yourself. Still maybe my experiences will help:

1. The fact that pea shoots are easy to grow and are the most versatile, being good both fresh and in cooked recipes, makes them a good soil sprout to start with. Plus they sell for $25.00 a pound at today's prices, which means there is potential for a good profit.

2. Sunflower greens are widely in demand, and the big hulls make them easy to pull off, but that's an extra step that must be done to offer a premium product. Unfortunately, I see bags of these greens in stores with the hulls left on and it's clear that this is the number one cause of the browning and all-around poor condition of

This shelf is holding a day's worth of trays, plus a shelf for my family, but it could hold fifty trays. Two cupboards like this is room for the one hundred trays—twenty-five trays a day to incubate in the dark. This is 36 inches wide and 44 inches high (91.4 × 111.8 cm). I adjust the shelves so they are 7 inches (17.8 cm) apart, so I have six shelves total. I fill three shelves and that will produce 6 pounds (2.7 kg) of shoots or soil sprouts every day.

those greens. There is no excuse for presenting sunflower greens with the hulls left on the seed leaf. Check the sunflower page (page 119) for tips on removing the hulls.

3. Basic buckwheat lettuce becomes dramatic looking when you take a little extra care to give it bright sunlight in the first day after incubation. The soil sprouts respond with a deeper red stem and a deep green leaf. It doesn't change basic buckwheat's flavor, but makes it a premium product; these colorful stems get everyone excited, and you can charge a good price for them. Some folks will buy buckwheat exclusively to use as a garnish with their regular salad greens. At times things have warranted repeating throughout this book and this is one of those times, so forgive me for the repetition, but you must make absolutely certain that you pick off the buckwheat hulls carefully. The best time to do this for buckwheat is before the shoots are cut. Double-check for straggling hulls during rinsing by pressing the

greens down into a bowl of water to let the hulls float to the top and pour them off, and then check them again while they are on the drying rack. While it is particularly crucial with buckwheat, this applies to all the shoots you sell; make sure they're cleaned carefully.

4. Broccoli greens are hard to find, they have a wealth of nutritional value, and the cole-family greens like purple kohlrabi make a beautiful addition to a salad, soup, or sandwich. One thing to consider with all of the cole family is that they are not as productive weight-wise, so you'll have to remember that if you want 4 ounces of broccoli sprouts, you'll have to plant two 4 inch by 8 inch (10.2 × 20.3 cm) trays. Also the seeds are much more expensive than peas, sunflower, and buckwheat, but you use only one-third as much seed for the same size tray, so check your pricing carefully to make sure the per-ounce price reflects your costs.

5. I would advise you to not mix your greens after they are cut. I know it is a common practice for farmers to plant and harvest single crops and then wash them in a tub or washing machine and mix them together in a barrel. It may be that tiny lettuces and microgreens are hardier than soil sprouts, but I doubt it. In my classes when we talk about buying microgreens, I hear the same complaint every time. You get home and find little black pieces of leaves that have started to turn almost immediately. I know when I buy them I busy myself picking the pieces out so they don't affect the rest and they don't end up in my salad. I am certain that it is the mixing process that creates this problem. Soil sprouts are no different; if the stem is broken in handling, it will brown at that spot first. You can see this after 4 days in the refrigerator. The cut end of the soil sprout will turn a little brown. For this reason I suggest that if you want to sell a mix, then grow it as a mix to start with because you will only have to handle the greens once, when you cut them off the tray and wash the whole batch. At least try it; I think you will agree that it makes a better product both in terms of freshness and how they look in the bag.

The Freshness Business

During my classes on indoor salad gardening, we talk about which greens are available in the produce section of local grocery stores. And as mentioned previously everyone who has ever bought a bag of premium mesclun or sprouts knows what it's like to get a bag home and find some of the leaves already starting to turn brown. After a day in the fridge some of the leaves are already turning black and starting to rot.

It's a big disappointment. Your soil sprouts will be fresher and last longer than these other greens. If you focus on presenting a consistent, high-quality product, you'll have loyal customers coming to you for greens. Your carefully cleaned produce will last a longer time in the refrigerator, as well.

Rinse your greens in cold, fresh water in shallow trays that fit the batch in order to conserve water. Pat them dry with a towel, or drain them on a slant board. They can be drained on a metal drying rack as well. Refrigerate the greens as soon as possible. I use 9 inch by 12 inch (22.9 × 30.5 cm) plastic bags that are FDA approved for food storage. On delivery day I keep the greens in a cooler with ice during transport. Put a piece of brown paper or cardboard between the ice and the bags of greens so they don't get frostbite.

Cut the greens to the same length when harvesting, keeping the stems aligned as much as possible. This makes them easier to clean, it's easier to pick off any hulls, and I think it makes a better-looking presentation on the shelf. It only takes a little care and organization to do this, and it's worth a lot in the end.

It's important to think about who you're marketing to and come up with a potential customer list to help develop your business. Here are some possibilities to get you started:

Two trays of pea shoots fill this 9 inch by 12 inch (22.9 × 30.5 cm) plastic bag with about 8 ounces (226.8 g) of greens.

1. *Small, specialty restaurants* (usually not big franchises) welcome these shoots for their menu. For instance there's a restaurant near me that serves a variety of healthy dishes, using as much local produce and local meats and breads as possible. They use shoots in a few of their daily dishes and as an option on all their sandwiches. Such places are perfect candidates to work with to sell your shoots. You might convince them to serve an all sprout salad as a regular menu item, too.

2. There's a great *coffee shop* in my town that serves the lunch crowd with an eclectic sandwich menu. Sprouts dress up everything, adding a nutritional boost as well as spectacular colors.

3. There are *health food stores* that are already familiar with offering fresh wheatgrass for juicing. You can grow wheatgrass easily, but you may find that the stores have sources in place and will be slow to change suppliers. However, they probably don't have suppliers for the shoots you'll offer; if they have a produce section, they'll likely welcome your bags of greens with open arms.

4. Most *food cooperatives* offer a variety of sprouts like alfalfa and mung beans. When you bring in your bags of fresh greens in beautiful colors, produce managers' eyes will pop. They'll want to know where they came from and where they can get more. Although many coops are being replaced by chains, plenty remain where you can sell your beautiful produce.

5. *Community-supported agriculture (CSA)* involves establishing a contract with your customers, who pay in advance for a supply of greens you deliver every week or so. Using a central delivery point such as a community center, farmers market, or a small general store, you provide a set amount of greens to each customer for a prepaid fee. Agreements can range from enough to feed a single person to greens for a large family, with offerings beginning at about 12 ounces (340.2 g) and going up to 3 pounds (1.4 kg) a week or more.

6. *Farmers markets* are great places to sell fresh greens. Bring along some of the greens growing in trays to make a showy display and satisfy a lot of the curiosity about the process. Most markets are conducted weekly on various days, so you might want to get into several of them with a few bags for each, rather than planting and harvesting huge amounts to market all at one time.

7. You might create a sideline *selling supplies* to people who want to grow their own soil sprouts. Don't be afraid that you'll lose business by doing this; these people often become your best customers and are good advertisement for your service.

8. *Bartering within your community* is another great option. If a local store owner wants to trade, you can take a store credit and shop

when you need to. It's like having a little savings account. Or you can just do a one-for-one swap for needed items in the old-fashioned way. However you barter it can be a lot of fun to work with your friends and neighbors.

9. *New money credits* is an intriguing concept that some organizations have promoted to restructure our society. The idea is to form an association with other services and providers and to bank credits whenever you provide someone in the network with your greens. Then you "spend" your credits when you get something from someone else in the system, such as a massage, homemade bread, or repairs for your car. Numerous links online will help you find or start an exchange network. If you search for "transition town" on the Internet, you may find an organization already started in your area, and it'll be a great resource.

10. Finally, consider *premaking tossed salads* for the grab-'n'-go section of your local coop or health food store. I know our local food cooperative has a popular selection for the lunch and dinner crowds looking for something wholesome and quick. A 4-ounce (113.4 g) salad is about the right size for a single serving and can be offered in a small plastic clamshell container. Or the store may want bags of mixed greens all ready to serve in their salad bar section.

This is where your creativity goes to work. Certainly in the winter months, when it is hard to find fresh, local organic greens, the lush shoots and colorful stems are a welcome sight. You will be surprised how easy it is to sell 6 pounds (2.7 kg) of greens every day.

The simple techniques of indoor salad gardening for growing large quantities of fresh greens are an important addition to efforts to localize our food production. It's not just the size of the operation that counts but its effectiveness in closing the loop of sustainable food resources.

This was one of the principles that prompted me to try expanding my indoor salad garden model for use in production farming in the first place. It is indeed possible, with elegant simplicity, to grow food for a family or a whole community, one windowsill at a time!

Acknowledgments

M y family deserves thanks for their patience and support in making this book become a reality. My wife, Deb, has been supportive in every way possible. My three sons, Michael, Dave, and Jake, have been encouraging and also great taste testers. Mike helped with the camera works and equipment. Dave built me an office that is enviable, with lots of shelves. Jake has been a huge help to me; when I was on crutches and needed someone to help me continue my classes and plant the trays, he was there and ended up learning the techniques well enough to say, "I could teach this class, Dad." After several months of sitting in on the classes, he was correcting me and adding things I forgot.

My two stepdaughters, Samantha Colt and Dr. Claudia Welch, have been supportive in the best way possible; they actually used the methods to grow fresh greens. Seeing them do it and enjoy their salads is the best kind of encouragement I could have received from them. Of course I believe it is Sam's husband, Chris Colt, who is the gardener in the family. It was a special pleasure to see Sam and her son, Sonny, nibbling on fresh pea shoots at breakfast. Claudia and her husband, Jim Ventresca, make room for trays of greens in their small living spaces. They sent pictures and created recipes that make this book a better resource.

My thanks to Samantha's daughters, Luna and Josie Colt, for help and encouragement. Josie helped me with classes by hauling the six boxes of stuff I need to present a class. I enjoyed seeing the light come on as she realized what this was all about. Her generation gets it—the need for sustainable living models. To you two, "Thank you."

When I first had the idea to give classes, my food local coop, Hunger Mountain Coop in Montpelier, Vermont, was very supportive and willing to help. Krystal (Owens) Fuller and Robyn Pierce have been just great in every way. Not only were they helpful with the logistics, but they were supportive of the idea of people growing their own greens. Also at the coop, Carmen Reyes helped me get seeds on the shelf of the store for enthusiastic students who wanted to take them home and plant their own trays of greens.

I received the same kind of help from the City Market in Burlington; they provided space and made arrangements for classes. I started working with Courtney Lange, and then Caroline Homan and Meg Klepak took over her spot. They were all helpful with the scheduling and hauling but also supportive of the idea. When I work with people like this, I am encouraged about the future; these people care. After one class at City Market, a lady said to the whole class, "This class has just saved me thousands of dollars." She was on her way to a local garden center to buy shelves with grow lights to raise her salad greens in her apartment; the tab for these shelves was about $1,500, so she was very pleased to learn these indoor salad gardening techniques.

After another class in Waitsfield for the Mad River Localvores, a nice young lady came up to me and asked, "Have you ever thought about writing a book? Have you thought about self-publishing?" It was a landmark moment for me. Loida and her husband, Tom Tham, have been encouraging and helpful in every way. They introduced me to then-president of the League of Vermont Writers, Pat O'Brien, who helped me initially write this book. To this team, thank you very much. Through them, I met author James Tabor, who gave me helpful advice on the tone of the book. I never realized that writing a book is a collaborative art. It really does take many able hands to create a book.

A shout out to my many garden buddies who have encouraged and helped me along the way: JR and his son in Geneva, Ohio; Ron Bouika in Wilkes-Barre, Pennsylvania; and Kathleen and her son in Woodbury, Vermont. Also to the whole gang in Maple Corner: Sarah Gallagher; Josie Connor; and Bob and Ginny, who grow the soil sprouts. Of course to Robin McDermot of the Mad River Localvores and Rose Nickerson of the Waterbury Garden Club. And teachers at U-32 High School, Steve Colangeli, Maggie Desch, and to Rick Hungerford, the director of U-32 Food Services, have been very supportive.

I would like to acknowledge the incredible team at Chelsea Green Publishing. Starting with Makenna Goodman, my editor, who started the ball rolling for me; I am grateful for her help to shape and expand the book. When Makenna told me she was leaving Chelsea Green to go on sabbatical, I was concerned that I was losing my champion; she 'got it' with my book. After a meeting with the whole group at the publisher's headquarters in White River Junction, Vermont, I came away with the clear message that they were in league with me and there was a remarkable bunch of talented people to create the finished volume and the market savvy to promote the book. Jenna Stewart and her assistant, Kirsten Wilson, contacted me about upcoming events to promote my book. Kalin Burhardt sent information about how to do the Amazon thing and gave me a list to complete the journey to become an author in today's world. I was blown away when I realized they had salesmen, Darrel Koerner and Michael Weaver, who would actually promote my book, in person, with industry leaders. It was fun to do the layout of the book with Pati Stone and Melissa Jacobson, who patiently listened to what was important to me in book presentation. Thanks to Christina Butt and Gretchen Kruesi, the marketing mavens. Hats off to Shay Totten, Communications Director, who made it simple that if I have a question and don't know who to talk with, call him to ensure an answer or get connected with the right person. Thanks to the whole team at Chelsea Green Publishers.

FAQ and Troubleshooting

Q: I think I have mold on my trays. How can I tell if it is mold, and what can I do about it?

A: This is the most common question I get in my classes and on my website. My son Jake always reminds me to address this in my classes, but if I forget, I hear about it later! What you are seeing is probably not mold but root hairs: the white fuzz surrounding a root. If it is mold, you will see a web of white hairs over the surface of the soil and usually brown on the stems. If you use the soil mix, mold will simply never happen. If you use garden soil or compost for the growing medium, it will happen frequently.

Q: Can I mix the seeds in the same tray?

A: Sure, I do it all the time. I have had some folks in my classes who swap seeds and plant a little of one and a little of another. I usually just mix the dry seeds before I soak them. Seed mixing is a lot of fun, so experiment.

Q: I read in the news that some people got sick from sprouts. What happened, and what can I do to protect myself?

A: This is a good question, and I hear it a lot and I understand your concern. When they talk about *E. coli* in the news, we pay attention. First the problem was not with soil sprouts, it was with alfalfa sprouts grown in a big industrial house. In these large operations the producers keep the seeds moist at all times, and the moist hulls stay right with the growing plants, versus the way soil sprouts grow so that they drop their hulls away from the greens and the hulls dry out. Second there has never been a case of *E. coli* or *Salmonella* in home-grown sprouts of any kind. For a home grower it is easy to wash the seeds before they are soaked, to pick off most of the hulls, and to wash the greens once they are cut. If you are still concerned, soak your seeds for 10 minutes in a 2 percent solution of chlorine before soaking them in plain water for planting.

Q: I forgot to water my plants, and they were wilted when I got home. Should I put holes in the trays and have a saucer of water under them like I have with my houseplants?

A: There are pictures of this in the book on page 24. As a matter of fact this has happened to me, so I can tell you what worked for me. I performed sprout CPR! I watered the tray and greens, put the tray in a plastic bag, and then put it in the fridge for a few hours—overnight was enough—and the tray revived to perfect greens. But you might want to give the plants a little more water at their daily watering if they are wilting that quickly. Usually they will be good if you miss just one day, but two days will be a problem.

Q: I don't have enough sunlight since there is no south-facing window in my apartment. Can I grow them under lights?

A: You can use lights, but you don't need them. Any window will give you adequate light for greening the young shoots. A bright sunny window is fine but not a necessity at all. Forget the lights; they are just an added expense.

Q: Can I use my own compost instead of buying compost?

A: You can use your own compost, but make sure it is at the bottom of the tray, and you might want to dehydrate the compost before you store it so you won't have critters hatching in your house or worms deciding to travel outside the tray!

Q: Can I grow in just compost?

A: I do not recommend this for two reasons. It will make for problems with mold, and it is too rich for these plants. Also the plants only need the small amount I recommend for fertilizer, and the soil structure in an only-compost growing medium is not the best for young seedlings; it can be crusty on top, which makes it hard for the tiny roots to penetrate. When growing seedlings for the outdoor garden, they are not grown in compost; it may be mixed in small amounts with the germination mix, but it is never used straight. So, taking a cue from nursery growers and from my own experience, I would discourage the idea.

Q: Can I use bird seed for the sunflower soil sprouts?

A: I do not use bird seed. I don't recommend it because it usually has a high percentage of rocks and stems, so it is not as good a deal as you think. Bird seed is usually not organic and it is frequently fumigated.

Q: What do I ask for when I go to get the soil mix you recommend?

A: Ask for a germination mix. It is about 80 percent peat moss; the rest is vermiculite, perlite, and limestone. Some have a growth enhancer that uses a mycorrhizal ingredient that actually grows a fungus on the root system and is supposed to do something to help the germinating plant grow. It is approved for organic gardening and seems to work, so if you find a germination mix that has this growth enhancer, it is OK to use. What you don't need is any fertilizer in the mix. Stay away from something called a hydro-gel, which is meant to hold moisture; this is for potted flowers in a hanging basket and is not for growing food. If you stick with the peat, vermiculite, and limestone, you can't go wrong.

Q: Why can't I use the good soil I have in my garden?

A: Even though the soil is good garden soil, it will likely crust up on the top and make it difficult for the roots to grow down into the dirt. As with compost it is probable that you will have mold kill your soil sprouts. Two good reasons to use the soil mix.

Q: How long do I have to let my radishes grow to become microgreens?

A: Microgreens are grown differently than soil sprouts, so soil sprouts will never become microgreens. In order to grow microgreens you must completely skip the 4 days of dark. They are grown in the light from the beginning.

Q: What can I do to keep my cats from eating my soil sprouts?

A: There are a few strategies I recommend. You can try to grow something they will like better, such as cat grass, which is really just wheatgrass with a fancy name. See the instructions on page 138 for wheatgrass. Another approach is to make the shelves you put your trays on too narrow for the cat to jump on and too high to bat with their paw. And the last idea, though it seems draconian, may be the best: Have a squirt bottle handy, particularly the very first time you set the soil sprouts on the windowsill, and give the cat a squirt the very first time it comes around to inspect them. This will give it the message that you do not want it near the sprouts right from the onset. I think this is easier than trying to discourage a cat after it has found a new toy.

Sources

Websites
The Daily Gardener
    www.thedailygardener.com
ISGA International Sprout Growers Association
    www.isga-sprouts.org/about-sprouts/nutritional-advantages
    -of-sprouts/
ISS International Specialty Supply
    www.sproutnet.com/sprouting-seed-varieties
Johns Hopkins University
  "Gutsy Germs Succumb to Baby Broccoli"
    www.hopkinsmedicine.org/news/media/releases/Gutsy_Germs
    _Succumb_to_Baby_Broccoli
  "Dietary Component Kills Bacterial Cause of Ulcers and Stomach
   Cancer: Laboratory Finding Points to Possible Economical Treat-
   ment of Infection"
    www.hopkinsmedicine.org/press/2002/may/020528.htm
USDA United Stated Department of Agriculture
    ndb.nal.usda.gov/ndb/foods/list

Books
*Balance Your Hormones, Balance Your Life: Achieving Optimal Health and
Wellness through Ayurveda, Chinese Medicine, and Western Science* (2011,
Da Capo Press)
    by Dr. Claudia Welch
*The Sprouting Book: How to Grow and Use Sprouts to Maximize Your
Health and Vitality* (1985, Avery Health Guides)
    by Ann Wigmore
Sproutman's Kitchen Garden Cookbook (1983, Sproutman Publications)
    by Steve Meyerowitz
SuperFoods Rx: Fourteen Foods that Will Change Your Life (2003,
William Morrow)
    by Steven G. Pratt and Kathy Matthews
Survival into the 21st Century: Planetary Healers Manual (1978, Twenty-
First Century Press)
    by Viktoras Kulvinskas

Index

Note: Page numbers in *italics* refer to photographs and figures;
page numbers followed by *t* refer to tables.

About the Author

Peter Burke started organic gardening at the young age of seventeen, inspired by the ideas he found in a new magazine, *Organic Farming and Gardening*. Peter has pursued a lifelong passion for organic gardening by reading everything he could find about gardening without chemicals and by trying many methods of gardening.

Peter expanded his gardening horizons when he worked for Viktoras Kulvinskas of the Hippocrates Health Institute in Boston. There he learned to grow all types of sprouts as well as wheatgrass and sunflower greens in large trays while tending the institute's organic garden.

In 1977, Peter settled with his family in Calais, Vermont—a difficult climate for gardening. A few years later he read the groundbreaking books *How to Grow More Vegetables* by John Jeavons and *Square Foot Gardening* by Mel Bartholomew, which introduced him to a completely new way to look at the craft of gardening. Rather than considering gardening as a miniature version of farming, Peter learned about the French Intensive methods started in Paris in 1890 and how to grow a lot more produce in much less space.

One of Peter's perennial frustrations of gardening in Vermont's short growing season was the lack of fresh salad greens from the garden through the long winters. In 2005, he set about trying to solve this problem, and by the end of that winter he had found the answer: his indoor soil sprouts method. Keen to confirm the methodology of his indoor salad gardening technique, he presented small classes at local food coops and garden clubs and then to larger groups at Gardener's Supply Company and NOFA-VT conferences in Burlingon, Vermont. His students confirm Peter's motto that "You can't mess this up": his method works for both the complete novice as well as the seasoned gardener.

Peter continues to live, garden, and write with his wife in Calais, Vermont.

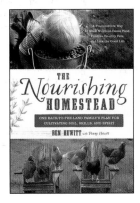

the politics and practice of sustainable living

CHELSEA GREEN PUBLISHING

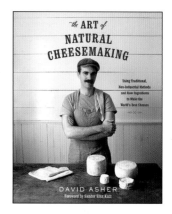

THE OCCIDENTAL ARTS & ECOLOGY CENTER COOKBOOK
Fresh-from-the-Garden Recipes for
Gatherings Large and Small
THE OAEC COLLECTIVE with OLIVIA RATHBONE
9781603585132
Hardcover • $40.00

THE ART OF NATURAL CHEESEMAKING
Using Traditional, Non-Industrial Methods and
Raw Ingredients to Make the World's Best Cheeses
DAVID ASHER
9781603585781
Paperback • $34.95

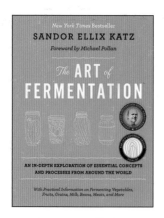

THE ART OF FERMENTATION
An In-Depth Exploration of Essential
Concepts and Processes from Around the World
SANDOR ELLIX KATZ
9781603582865
Hardcover • $39.95

MAKE MEAD LIKE A VIKING
Traditional Techniques for Brewing Natural,
Wild-Fermented, Honey-Based Wines and Beers
JEREME ZIMMERMAN
9781603585989
Paperback • $24.95

the politics and practice of sustainable living

For more information or to request a catalog,
visit **www.chelseagreen.com** or
call toll-free **(800) 639-4099**.